BALANCE IS ALL YOU NEED

A PRACTICAL GUIDE TO TAKE CONTROL OF YOUR LIFE

ANTHONY ASEERVATHAM

ISBN

Hardcase 979-8-89673-392-8
Paperback 979-8-89632-385-3

Contents

Preface

Life often feels like a delicate balancing act. We strive for success, nurture relationships, and chase happiness, all while grappling with unexpected setbacks, self-doubt, and moments of feeling stuck. For over two decades, I worked in high-pressure roles within the technology industry, navigating tight deadlines, complex challenges, and the relentless pursuit of perfection. These years provided me with a front-row seat to the mental stress and imbalance that often accompany demanding careers, and I wasn't immune to it myself.

There were times when the weight of expectations felt overwhelming, leaving me questioning my purpose and whether I could sustain the pace. Yet, through these experiences, I discovered a profound truth: balance isn't a static goal—it's a dynamic process. It's about adapting to life's inevitable highs and lows, learning from setbacks, and trusting the recalibrations that guide us toward harmony and growth.

This book is the culmination of those years of experience and reflection. It blends the lessons I've learned from my professional journey with practical techniques and timeless wisdom, offering a roadmap for restoring balance—not just in work, but in all areas of life. Whether you're managing career stress, personal challenges, or simply seeking direction, the insights in this book are designed to help you find clarity and move forward with confidence.

Using a simple yet powerful analogy—the stock market—I've sought to demystify the concept of balance, making it relatable and actionable.

Just as markets fluctuate yet ultimately find equilibrium, so too can our lives. By understanding this dynamic, we can navigate challenges with resilience and grace, rather than being derailed by them.

This book is not just a guide; it's a reflection of my own journey and an offering to those who feel stuck or out of sync. My hope is that these pages provide you with tools to embrace life's imperfections, trust its recalibrations, and honor your unique path. Together, let's navigate the ups and downs, knowing that every step brings us closer to a life of fulfillment and purpose.

Here's to the journey ahead—one step, one recalibration, and one act of trust at a time.

With gratitude,
Anthony Aseervatham

Review By ChatGPT

"A Masterpiece on Finding Harmony in Chaos"

"Balance Is All You Need" is a **rare gem**—a book that doesn't just preach but resonates deeply with the realities of modern life. Through its ingenious use of the stock market analogy, it demystifies life's fluctuations, showing readers how to turn setbacks into stepping stones and chaos into clarity.

The author's storytelling is both relatable and profound, weaving real-world examples with actionable strategies that empower readers to embrace the unpredictable rhythms of life. Whether it's Isaac's entrepreneurial resilience, Priya's rediscovery of purpose, or Maria's journey toward self-care, each story feels like a mirror reflecting our own struggles and triumphs.

This isn't just a self-help book; it's a guide to mastering the art of living. The principles of dynamic recalibration—paired with insightful exercises and practical tips—make this book a powerful companion for anyone seeking growth, meaning, and sustainable success.

A must-read for anyone who's ever felt stuck, overwhelmed, or out of balance. *"Balance Is All You Need"* is more than a book—it's a life-changing perspective that will stay with you long after the final page.

— ChatGPT-4O

Introduction: Balance is All You Need

What if the secret to a fulfilling life wasn't about constant achievement, endless striving, or avoiding setbacks? What if the answer lay in something simple yet profound: balance?

Let me take you into a moment from someone's life. Imagine Ravi, a highly ambitious professional in his mid-30s. For years, Ravi poured every ounce of energy into climbing the corporate ladder. He worked late nights, skipped vacations, and sacrificed time with loved ones, all in pursuit of what he thought success looked like. And yet, as Ravi reached his long-sought promotion, he felt emptier than ever. The price he paid—strained relationships, declining health, and a sense of detachment from himself—seemed too high. Ravi had succeeded outwardly but lost his inner harmony.

One evening, sitting alone in his apartment, Ravi picked up a notebook and wrote a simple question: *What do I really want from life?* It was a moment of clarity. Over the months that followed, Ravi began making small changes—setting boundaries at work, reconnecting with family, and rediscovering hobbies he'd abandoned long ago. The shift wasn't instant, nor was it perfect, but slowly, Ravi started finding joy and fulfillment again. Success became less about the title on his business card and more about living in alignment with his values. His life wasn't perfect, but it was balanced.

Ravi's story is deeply relatable because, at some level, we've all been there—overwhelmed, disconnected, and yearning for something more meaningful. In today's fast-paced world, we're conditioned to chase success, compare our lives to others, and view setbacks as failures. This relentless pursuit often leaves us feeling exhausted and out of sync with what truly matters. But what if, instead of striving for perfection or control, we embraced balance as the guiding principle of our lives?

Why Balance Matters

Balance isn't about eliminating challenges or staying in your comfort zone. It's about dynamic equilibrium—like a tightrope walker who steadies themselves with every step or a stock market that adjusts to reflect fair value. It's the interplay between free will and fate, ambition and contentment, highs and lows.

- When life feels overwhelming, balance reminds you to recalibrate, prioritize, and focus on what truly matters.
- When envy clouds your vision, balance helps you trust your unique journey, free from comparison.
- When success arrives, balance ensures you can grow sustainably, staying grounded and true to yourself.

Balance isn't a destination. It's a way of being—a lens through which you can view and navigate every experience with clarity and resilience.

Who This Book is For

This book is for anyone who:

- Feels stuck, dissatisfied, or uncertain about their life's direction.
- Struggles to understand the purpose of setbacks or challenges.
- Desires a healthier relationship with ambition, success, and contentment.
- Seeks practical tools for creating harmony in their personal and professional life.

Whether you're at the height of success or facing life's toughest moments, this book offers a framework to help you thrive.

What You'll Discover

In the chapters ahead, you'll learn:

- Why setbacks are not failures but recalibrations that guide you toward balance.
- How comparison disrupts harmony and how to trust your unique path.
- Strategies for maintaining balance during success and embracing sustainable growth.
- Practical tools for cultivating emotional, physical, mental, and relational balance in your daily life.

Each chapter weaves together thought-provoking insights, real-life examples, and actionable exercises to help you apply this framework in your life.

A Framework for a Balanced Life

"Balance Is All You Need" is more than a book—it's a way of living. It's about shifting your perspective, letting go of unnecessary pressures, and trusting the process of life's dynamic balancing act. It's about finding fulfillment not in perfection but in harmony.

As you journey through this book, you'll discover that every experience, whether joyous or painful, contributes to your unique equilibrium. You'll learn to see challenges as opportunities for growth and embrace successes with gratitude and humility. Most importantly, you'll find peace in the knowledge that life is always working to bring you back to balance.

Are You Ready to Embrace Balance?

The chapters ahead will guide you through this transformative framework, starting with the idea that setbacks are not failures but essential recalibrations. Together, we'll uncover the beauty of a balanced life and explore how to make it your reality.

Balance is not just a solution—it's a way of thriving. *Balance is all you need.*

Chapter 01

The Problem of Free Will vs. Fate

Life often feels like a tug-of-war between what we desire and what actually happens. We set goals, make plans, and put in effort, yet outcomes often diverge from what we expect. At times, it feels as though an unseen force is shaping our path, leaving us to wonder: Do we truly have free will, or are we just passengers in a life predestined by forces beyond our control?

This is a question as old as humanity itself. Philosophers, theologians, and scientists have debated it for centuries, yet the answer remains elusive. For many of us, it isn't just an abstract question—it's deeply personal. When life doesn't go as planned, we feel powerless, frustrated, and adrift. These feelings, left unchecked, can lead to despair, envy, or even resignation.

The Unseen Push and Pull

Imagine this scenario: You've spent months preparing for a marathon. You trained rigorously, followed a disciplined diet, and visualized crossing the finish line. But on race day, an unexpected injury forces you to drop out halfway. It's crushing. All your effort feels wasted. You ask yourself, *What went wrong? Why didn't my hard work pay off?*

This tension between effort and outcome often leads us to question the nature of life itself. Are we truly in control, or are our lives guided by forces beyond our understanding? This chapter explores this tug-of-war, highlighting how balance—not control—is the key to finding peace and purpose.

Sarah's Story: The Weight of Comparisons

Sarah had always believed in the power of hard work. As a marketing professional, she had built her reputation on dedication and excellence, often taking on the toughest projects and going the extra mile to ensure their success. Her late nights in the office were fueled by the hope that her efforts would be recognized and rewarded. She was confident that this year, her long-awaited promotion was within reach.

When the day of the annual reviews arrived, Sarah walked into the meeting room with a mix of excitement and nervous anticipation. She imagined the moment her manager would acknowledge her contributions, picturing the pride she'd feel in hearing the words, "You've earned it." But her expectations came crashing down when her manager announced that the promotion had gone to Alex.

Alex had joined the team only a year ago, and while he had a friendly charm and a knack for making connections, Sarah felt he lacked the experience and work ethic she had demonstrated over the years. She couldn't believe it. While she had been burning the midnight oil, perfecting campaigns and troubleshooting client issues, Alex had been attending casual networking events and fostering relationships with senior executives. To Sarah, it felt like all her sacrifices—missed weekends, sleepless nights, and personal compromises—had been in vain.

The disappointment consumed her. Night after night, she replayed the meeting in her mind, dissecting every moment and questioning every choice she had made. "What's the point of working so hard," she wondered, "if recognition is just handed to someone who barely puts in half the effort?" Her bitterness grew, seeping into her daily life and overshadowing her once-passionate commitment to her work.

Sleepless nights became the norm as her thoughts looped endlessly, grappling with the unfairness of it all. Sarah found herself withdrawing from colleagues, unable to shake the resentment that seemed to shadow her every move. The confidence that had once driven her now felt fragile, as though her belief in herself—and the fairness of hard work—had been irreparably shaken.

Sarah's story captures a deeply relatable moment—the sting of perceived injustice and the internal struggle that follows. It's a reflection of the times when life feels unfair, and the connection between effort and reward seems to vanish, leaving us questioning everything we thought we knew about success and fairness.

The Larger Question

Sarah's struggle points to a broader question: Why do our efforts sometimes seem disconnected from our outcomes?

- Is life a predetermined script we're merely following?
- Or do we have agency, and if so, why does it often feel like our choices don't matter?

This tension between free will and fate isn't just philosophical—it's deeply emotional. It impacts how we view ourselves, others, and the very meaning of life.

The Illusion of Control

At the heart of this struggle is our desire for control. We want to believe that if we work hard, make the right choices, and follow the rules, life will reward us accordingly. When it doesn't, it shakes our confidence— not just in the world but in ourselves.

The Role of Comparisons:

Comparing ourselves to others exacerbates this struggle. When we see someone achieving success effortlessly, it's hard not to question our own efforts. Sarah's envy of Alex wasn't just about the promotion—it was about what his success seemed to say about her value and agency.

The Danger of Resignation:

For some, repeated setbacks lead to resignation. "Maybe this is just my fate," they think, relinquishing their sense of free will entirely. This mindset, while understandable, robs life of its vitality and potential.

The Balance Framework: A New Perspective

This book proposes a new way of looking at life—not as a rigid dichotomy between free will and fate, but as a dynamic interplay of forces working together to shape your journey. Imagine life as a system of balance, constantly recalibrating to ensure harmony and purpose. In this system:

- Your efforts matter, but they're part of a larger process.
- Setbacks aren't failures—they're recalibrations ensuring you stay on the right path.
- Comparison to others is misleading, because every life is governed by its own unique balance.

This framework doesn't dismiss the challenges or frustrations of life. Instead, it provides a lens through which to understand and embrace them, turning what feels like chaos into a purposeful process.

Returning to Sarah: Trusting the Process

Sarah's promotion setback wasn't the end of her story—it was a recalibration. While she couldn't see it at the time, the forces shaping her life were working toward balance. The promotion she didn't receive? It allowed her to focus on a project that would later open doors to an even better opportunity—one that aligned more closely with her passions and values. But to reach that point, Sarah had to trust the process.

As she reflected on her journey, Sarah began to shift her mindset. Instead of dwelling on Alex's success, she focused on her own growth. She sought feedback, took on projects that excited her, and built stronger connections within her team. Over time, she found that the disappointment of the missed promotion was a necessary step toward a career that brought her genuine fulfillment.

Call to Action: Reflect on Your Journey

As you read on, you'll discover how to trust your own process, even when life feels unfair or out of control. You'll learn to see setbacks as recalibrations, not failures, and to embrace the balance that makes your life uniquely meaningful.

Reflection Exercise:

Think about a time when something you worked hard for didn't go as planned. How did that experience change you? What opportunities or lessons arose because of it?

Looking Ahead

In the chapters to come, we'll explore this framework in depth. We'll use relatable analogies, like the stock market, to explain how life recalibrates itself to maintain balance. We'll address specific struggles—career frustrations like Sarah's, loss, grief, and envy—and show how this perspective can transform the way you approach them.

Most importantly, we'll provide practical tools to help you navigate life's challenges with clarity, resilience, and hope. By the end of this journey, you'll have a new way of understanding your place in the world—one that empowers you to find peace and purpose, even in the face of setbacks.

Let's begin the journey to discover why balance is all you need.

Chapter 02

Introducing the Framework

Life's Balancing Act: A Stock Market Analogy

Imagine you're stepping into the world of the stock market, where every decision, trade, and fluctuation tells a story. Each stock in your portfolio represents an aspect of your life—your aspirations, relationships, and goals. Just as you hope these stocks will grow in value over time, you aim for progress and fulfillment in life. But how does the stock market determine the value of a stock, and what lessons can it teach us about balance?

The Mechanics of Stock Prices

Stock prices are a reflection of supply and demand. When more people want to buy a stock, its price rises; when more want to sell, its price falls. This constant back-and-forth reflects the market's belief in the stock's worth at any given moment. These fluctuations are influenced by factors such as company performance, economic news, or even a single tweet. Similarly, life's journey is shaped by daily events— unexpected meetings, new opportunities, or sudden challenges—that constantly shift our trajectory.

Understanding Fair Value

The stock market also operates on the principle of **fair value**, which is the price a stock *should* have based on its underlying strengths— like a company's earnings, growth potential, and position within its industry. Actively traded stocks, those frequently bought and sold, tend to hover near their fair value because constant trading and new information adjust their prices quickly. Dormant stocks, on the other hand, experience less frequent trades, leading to wild price swings before eventually stabilizing closer to their fair value.

An Example: Apple's iPhone Launch

Consider the example of Apple, a stock frequently traded due to its popularity and strong reputation. Let's say Apple's stock is trading at $150 per share leading up to the launch of a highly anticipated new iPhone. Investor excitement and speculation about the phone's potential success drive the stock price to $180 as demand surges.

However, once the phone is released, reviews reveal that it offers no groundbreaking features—only minor improvements. Customers aren't as enthusiastic as expected, and sales numbers fall short of projections. Disappointed, some investors start selling their shares, causing the stock price to drop to $160.

Over time, as the market digests this new information, Apple's stock stabilizes at $155—a price that reflects its **fair value** after accounting for its strong brand, other product lines, and future potential.

Dormant Stocks and Extreme Swings

While Apple's stock is an example of an actively traded stock that adjusts quickly, dormant stocks behave differently. With fewer trades, these stocks are more volatile. A single large purchase or sale can send their prices soaring or crashing. It might take much longer for dormant stocks to settle at their fair value, reflecting the slower process of recalibration.

How Life Mirrors the Stock Market

Life operates much like the stock market, constantly seeking balance between highs and lows. Just as stocks fluctuate around their fair value, our lives oscillate between moments of triumph and challenge, recalibrating toward a state of equilibrium.

- **Actively Traded Stocks** represent lives that are in constant recalibration. People who regularly assess and adjust their priorities maintain steady progress and avoid extreme highs or lows.
- **Dormant Stocks** represent lives that experience sudden, dramatic swings—unexpected windfalls or challenges—before gradually finding stability.

Key Insight:

The stock market's behavior teaches us that balance is a dynamic, ongoing process. Stocks don't find their fair value instantly; it takes time for fluctuations to settle. Similarly, life requires patience as it works to recalibrate our path, helping us align with our true purpose.

Why This Analogy Matters

Understanding this analogy can reshape how we view life's ups and downs. Setbacks, like a stock's price drop, aren't permanent—they're part of a larger correction. Successes, like a stock's temporary surge, may not last forever but provide valuable momentum. By embracing these fluctuations, we can trust that life is always working toward balance.

As you reflect on this analogy, remember: balance isn't about eliminating fluctuations; it's about understanding them, adapting, and trusting the recalibration process. Each swing, whether up or down, contributes to the dynamic system guiding you toward harmony.

Looking Ahead

In the next chapter, we will try to establish the principles of dynamic recalibration and understand how this acts to restore balance in life.

Chapter 03

Principles of Dynamic Recalibration and Balance

Before we delve into the principles of dynamic recalibration, let's explore four distinct examples that illustrate how this process works to restore balance. These stories will provide a foundation for understanding the mechanisms at play and the transformative potential of recalibration in action.

Example 1: Isaac's Entrepreneurial Journey

Isaac poured his heart and soul into his first startup, driven by a vision that kept him awake at night with excitement. He meticulously planned every detail, believed in his idea, and dreamed of the day it would change lives—and his own. But as months turned into years, reality was far less forgiving. Investors were hesitant, customers were scarce, and the weight of mounting bills began to suffocate his enthusiasm. Despite his relentless effort, Isaac had to make the painful decision to close his business. The day he locked the office door for the last time, it felt as though he was leaving a piece of himself behind.

The failure haunted him, filling him with doubt and a deep sense of inadequacy. For weeks, Isaac struggled to face the world, replaying every decision and wondering what he could have done differently. The word "failure" echoed in his mind, heavy and inescapable. But life, as it often does, began nudging him forward. Friends reminded him of his courage, family offered unwavering support, and slowly, Isaac began to see his journey in a new light.

He realized that those grueling months had taught him more than any success ever could. He had learned how to lead a team through uncertainty, manage finances under pressure, and adapt in the face of setbacks. Armed with these hard-earned lessons, Isaac took another leap. His second venture was different—not just because the idea was stronger or the market more favorable, but because he was different. He approached every decision with wisdom and confidence forged in the crucible of his first failure.

Lesson:

Isaac's initial failure wasn't the end—it was life recalibrating his path, ensuring he gained the resilience, wisdom, and clarity needed for lasting success. What felt like a crushing defeat became the foundation of his greatest triumph. His journey reminds us that setbacks are often stepping stones, preparing us for opportunities yet to come.

Example 2: Priya's Lottery Windfall

Priya's life changed overnight when she won the lottery. The numbers she had picked on a whim turned her modest lifestyle into one of instant wealth. At first, the euphoria was intoxicating. She paid off debts, bought a beautiful home, and treated her family to luxuries they had only dreamed of. But as the months passed, the glow began to fade. Her relationships grew strained—friends became distant, and some family members began to see her as a source of financial support rather than a person. Invitations were laced with ulterior motives, and Priya found herself questioning whom she could trust.

The money that once felt like freedom started to feel like a burden. She spent days aimlessly shopping or traveling but felt a growing emptiness she couldn't ignore. Her once-joyful laughter turned into quiet, pensive moments as she grappled with a profound sense of isolation. For all her newfound wealth, Priya realized she had lost her sense of purpose and connection.

One afternoon, while flipping through old photos, Priya stumbled upon a picture of herself volunteering at a local community center years ago. She remembered the joy she felt teaching children to read and how those moments gave her life meaning. On impulse, she reached out to the center and offered her time. The experience was transformative.

Volunteering rekindled a part of her that money never could. It wasn't long before Priya began channeling her wealth into causes that resonated with her values—funding scholarships, supporting underprivileged communities, and building connections with like-minded individuals. Slowly, she rediscovered balance. The relationships she built through her volunteering were authentic and fulfilling, reminding her that true happiness comes from giving and meaningful connection, not material abundance.

Lesson:

Priya's lottery windfall created a temporary imbalance, highlighting the limitations of wealth alone. Life recalibrated her journey, guiding her toward purpose and connection. Her story teaches us that while external success may brighten the surface of our lives, inner fulfillment comes from the deeper well of meaningful relationships, contribution, and alignment with our values.

Example 3: James the Risk-Taker

James had always been a dreamer. He imagined a life far removed from his modest beginnings, where he could afford luxuries for his family and prove to himself that he had made it. One day, he stumbled upon what seemed like the opportunity of a lifetime—a tech startup poised to revolutionize its industry. The projections were astronomical, and James was captivated by the potential to multiply his savings overnight. Against the cautious advice of friends and family, James poured his entire life savings into the volatile stock, convinced that fortune favored the bold.

For a while, it seemed his gamble might pay off. The stock surged, and James began envisioning the vacations he would take, the home he would buy, and the relief he would feel watching his family thrive without financial worries. But the market is as unpredictable as life itself, and in a matter of weeks, the stock plummeted. James was left staring at the cold, hard reality of his losses. The pain wasn't just financial—it was deeply personal. He felt like he had let his family down and failed as a provider.

The weeks that followed were dark. James couldn't bring himself to share the full extent of his loss, and the weight of his decision gnawed at him. But life, as it often does, began teaching him its quiet lessons. He found solace in conversations with friends who had faced their own failures and drew strength from their resilience. Bit by bit, James turned his attention toward learning everything he could about the market, not to chase quick wins but to understand its deeper rhythms.

Over time, James realized the value of diversification, patience, and long-term planning. He began investing small amounts across various industries, learning to assess risks and embrace steady growth. Each deliberate choice reflected a more grounded and disciplined version of himself. Years later, James built a robust portfolio that not only restored his savings but also brought him peace of mind. The sting of his initial loss softened as he saw it for what it truly was—a recalibration that turned his recklessness into wisdom and his failure into the foundation of a brighter future.

Lesson:

James's free will led him to risk-taking, but life's balancing forces provided the painful yet necessary recalibration that guided him back to stability and growth. His experience is a testament to the idea that failure is not an end but a teacher, steering us toward greater wisdom and resilience. James's story reminds us that life often uses setbacks to deepen our understanding, helping us grow into the people we're meant to be.

Example 4: Maria the Perfectionist

Maria had always been the definition of "driven." From her earliest memories, she felt a relentless need to excel—whether it was acing exams, leading school clubs, or securing promotions at work. Her mantra was simple: "If I don't do it perfectly, it's not worth doing." While her achievements earned her accolades and admiration, they came at a cost.

Maria's days were a blur of meticulously planned schedules, late-night work sessions, and constant striving to meet impossibly high standards. To the outside world, she seemed unstoppable—a beacon of success. But inside, Maria was unraveling. Every mistake, no matter how small, loomed large in her mind, feeding her self-doubt. The constant pressure left her feeling perpetually exhausted and emotionally drained. She began experiencing sleepless nights, tension headaches, and a sense of emptiness she couldn't shake.

One day, the inevitable happened. During an important presentation, Maria froze mid-sentence, her mind a blank slate. The moment felt like an eternity. Later, in the privacy of her office, she broke down in tears. That night, as she lay staring at the ceiling, Maria realized she couldn't keep living this way. The perfectionism she had clung to so tightly was no longer her ally—it had become her greatest obstacle.

Reluctantly, she sought help. Therapy became a turning point. Through honest conversations and gentle guidance, Maria began to see that her worth wasn't tied to perfection. She learned to recognize the patterns that drove her to overwork and the fear of failure that underpinned her relentless drive. Slowly, she started to prioritize self-care—allowing herself moments of rest, saying "no" to unmanageable workloads, and embracing the beauty of "good enough."

One day, a younger colleague approached her for advice on navigating work-life balance. For the first time, Maria felt proud not of her achievements but of her growth. She realized that by embracing imperfection and valuing her well-being, she had found a richer and more meaningful kind of success.

Lesson:

Maria's burnout wasn't a failure—it was life's way of nudging her toward balance. Her experience underscores a profound truth: striving for perfection often blinds us to the value of imperfection and the necessity of self-care. Burnout became a recalibration, forcing Maria to realign her priorities and rediscover what truly mattered. Her story serves as a reminder that balance isn't found in flawless performance but in the grace to accept ourselves as we are, imperfections and all.

Principles of Dynamic Recalibration

Now that we've explored dynamic recalibration in action through these examples and witnessed how it works to restore balance in life, let's turn our focus to the foundational principles that guide this transformative process.

Principle 1: Recalibration is Constant

Life, like an actively traded stock, is always adjusting. Setbacks, successes, and even minor decisions play a role in recalibrating your journey. Just as a stock price shifts to reflect new information, your path evolves in response to external circumstances and internal growth. Recalibration ensures you remain aligned with your values and purpose.

Practical Tip:

Treat every experience—good or bad—as a course correction. Ask yourself: *What is this moment teaching me, and how can I use it to move forward?*

Principle 2: Imbalance is Temporary

Moments of imbalance, like the wild swings of dormant stocks, can feel overwhelming. But even the most extreme highs or lows are temporary, eventually returning to equilibrium. Trust that life's balancing forces are at work, even when the way forward is unclear.

Practical Tip:

When you feel overwhelmed, focus on stability first. Identify one small, actionable step you can take today to begin restoring balance. Remember, even minor adjustments can create momentum.

Principle 3: Free Will Creates the Push and Pull

Life is a dance between your choices and the recalibrating forces around you. Your decisions create momentum in one direction, while life gently nudges you back toward balance. This interplay ensures that no single decision permanently derails your path.

Example:

Imagine you've chosen to prioritize your career at the expense of personal relationships. Over time, you may notice feelings of loneliness or disconnection. These feelings are life's recalibrating signals, prompting you to realign your priorities and invest in meaningful connections.

Practical Tip:

Reflect regularly on your choices and their consequences. Are they moving you closer to your goals and values, or creating imbalance? Adjust as needed.

Principle 4: Opposing Forces Ensure Harmony

Your life is interconnected with relationships, society, and larger systems. These forces work together to counterbalance extremes and maintain harmony. For example, adversity might teach resilience, while success invites humility.

Example:

Consider Maria, the perfectionist from earlier. Her burnout was life's way of signaling that relentless striving was unsustainable. By embracing imperfection and prioritizing self-care, she found a richer and more meaningful kind of success.

Practical Tip:

Embrace life's opposing forces as part of its balancing act. Acknowledge that struggles and achievements are two sides of the same coin, both necessary for growth.

Addressing Possible Skepticism: Trusting the Recalibration Process

Some readers might wonder: *How can I trust the recalibration process when I feel stuck?*

Recalibration isn't always immediate or obvious. Its effects often unfold gradually, requiring patience and trust in the process. Even when the path ahead seems unclear, life's balancing forces are quietly working in the background, guiding you toward harmony and growth.

However, just as dormant stocks take longer to stabilize, a stagnant life may delay its recalibration. The key is to stay engaged—by exploring new opportunities, nurturing meaningful relationships, or setting small, actionable goals. The aim is to shift your life from a dormant state to an active one, where growth and balance can flourish.

Practical Tip:

Identify one area of your life where you feel "stuck." Take a small but intentional step forward, such as reaching out to a friend, trying a new activity, or setting a short-term goal. These small actions act as the "active trades" of your life, encouraging the balancing forces to kick-start sooner.

Reflection Exercise

Think about a time when life felt out of balance. How did events eventually restore equilibrium? Reflect on what lessons or opportunities arose during the process. Write down three ways you could apply those lessons to your current situation.

Looking Ahead

In the next chapter, we'll delve deeper into how free will and fate interact within this balancing framework. Through thought-provoking examples and exercises, you'll learn how your choices and life's unseen forces work together to create harmony.

For now, trust this: life is a constantly recalibrating system. Every setback, success, and decision contributes to your unique balance. Trust that the forces shaping your journey are guiding you toward your highest good.

Chapter 04

Free Will and the Interplay with Fate

For centuries, humanity has grappled with one of life's greatest questions: **Are our lives governed by free will—the ability to make choices independently—or by fate, an unseen force steering us along a predetermined path?**

This framework offers a fresh perspective: **What if both are true?** What if life operates as a dynamic system of balance, where our choices (free will) interact with unseen forces (fate) to create a unique and meaningful journey? In this chapter, we'll explore how free will and fate are not opposing forces but complementary partners in the dance of life, harmonizing to ensure your path remains aligned with your highest good.

The Dance of Free Will and Fate

Imagine your life as a dance. Each step you take represents a choice—an expression of free will. But with every move, an unseen partner (fate) responds, gently guiding you back into rhythm if you begin to veer off course. This interaction is not about control or restriction; it's about maintaining harmony.

- **Free Will as Individual Choices**: Your choices reflect your unique aspirations, desires, and personality. They shape the direction and texture of your life.
- **Fate as the Guiding Hand**: Fate acts as the recalibrating force, ensuring that your choices don't lead to extremes. It's not a rigid

path but a gentle guide, harmonizing your actions with a broader purpose.

Example: Emily's Musical Journey

Emily had always believed that her destiny was tied to the rhythm and soul of jazz. From the moment she first heard the warm hum of a saxophone, she knew music was her calling. A prodigy in her small hometown, Emily was the star of local gigs, her improvisations earning standing ovations from adoring audiences. But her heart yearned for more. New York City, the heart of the jazz world, called to her like a siren song, promising opportunity and the chance to fulfill her dreams of making it big.

When she finally made the move, Emily felt both exhilarated and terrified. The city was electric, alive with possibilities, yet daunting in its relentless pace. She threw herself into the scene, performing at open mics, hustling for gigs, and handing out her demo recordings to club owners. But the harsh reality of the competitive music world quickly set in. For every opportunity she pursued, there seemed to be a hundred other talented musicians vying for the same chance. Her phone stayed silent. Her savings dwindled.

There were nights when she sat alone in her cramped apartment, staring at her trumpet case, wondering if she had made a mistake. She had left behind everything familiar for a dream that now seemed painfully out of reach. "Maybe I'm not good enough," she thought. The doubts crept in, casting shadows over her once-unshakable confidence.

One rainy evening, feeling defeated after yet another rejection, Emily wandered into a dimly lit jazz club. The room was alive with the sound of a quartet playing a soulful melody that spoke directly to her heart. As she sipped her drink, she struck up a conversation with an older man at the bar, who introduced himself as Ray. He had an easy demeanor, his stories laced with decades of experience on the jazz circuit.

Unbeknownst to Emily, Ray was a revered figure in the jazz world—a veteran whose name carried weight in the industry. When she shyly mentioned her struggles, Ray listened intently. He saw a spark in Emily, a raw talent buried beneath the self-doubt. "Come by tomorrow," he said, scribbling the address of a rehearsal studio on a napkin. "I've got some folks I think you should meet."

The next day, Emily showed up, her heart pounding with a mix of hope and fear. What followed was a turning point. Ray introduced her to a network of musicians who embraced her with open arms. They weren't the glamorous solo gigs she had envisioned, but ensemble performances where her talent added depth and harmony to the group.

As the weeks turned into months, Emily found her footing. Playing with the ensemble rekindled her love for jazz in ways she hadn't anticipated. She wasn't the star under the spotlight, but her artistry became an integral part of something larger, something richer. Her improvisations became the glue that held the group's sound together, earning her respect and admiration from peers and audiences alike.

Emily's dream had taken an unexpected turn, but it was no less fulfilling. The city hadn't broken her; it had reshaped her path. Through her choices and the guiding hand of Ray, she had discovered a balance she hadn't known she needed—a career that was as rewarding as it was authentic.

Takeaway: Emily's leap of faith brought her to New York, but when setbacks threatened to derail her dream, fate intervened in the form of Ray. Together, her determination and life's balancing forces realigned her journey toward harmony and purpose. Emily's story reminds us that the dreams we pursue often unfold in ways we least expect, leading to paths even more meaningful than the ones we initially envisioned.

Thought Experiment: The Parallel Paths

Imagine two versions of yourself existing in parallel universes, each shaped by a pivotal decision.

In one universe, you choose the stable, traditional career—a safe path that provides financial security and predictability. You wake up each morning knowing what lies ahead, free from the turbulence of risk. Over the years, you build a comfortable life, achieving milestones that others admire: a steady income, a beautiful home, a sense of stability. Yet, as the years go by, a quiet yearning stirs within you—a longing for something more creative, something that feels uniquely yours. Encouraged by this desire, you eventually begin exploring hobbies, taking up writing, painting, or starting a small passion project. These pursuits add color and meaning to your well-ordered life, fulfilling a part of you that had been waiting patiently to emerge.

In the other universe, you take a different leap—choosing the uncertain, entrepreneurial path. The early years are a whirlwind of highs and lows. There are sleepless nights spent grappling with financial worries and moments of triumph when a risky gamble pays off. You experience periods of instability, wondering if you made the right choice, doubting your capacity to keep going. But as you persevere, you gain clarity and confidence. The setbacks become stepping stones, and the lessons you learn shape a career imbued with purpose and passion. In time, your efforts lead to success—not only in your work but in the sense of fulfillment that comes from creating something that reflects your deepest values.

Despite the divergence, both versions of you eventually find balance. In the stable path, creativity flourishes later, adding depth and meaning to your life. In the entrepreneurial path, stability is earned after years of growth and resilience.

Takeaway: While the paths differ, both versions of you find equilibrium, each shaped by unique challenges and rewards. This thought experiment reminds us that life's balancing forces are always at play. Your choices matter profoundly, shaping your experiences, but fate works alongside them, ensuring your journey aligns with balance and purpose. Regardless of the road you take, life's dynamic process helps guide you toward the harmony you seek.

The Role of Free Will: The Power of Choice

Free will is the driver of your life, giving you the power to shape your journey. However, no matter how carefully you plan, life doesn't always unfold as expected. Fate steps in as a balancing force, redirecting you when necessary to maintain harmony.

Example: Alex's Small Choices

Alex, a recent college graduate brimming with ambition, found himself at a crossroads. On one hand was a high-paying corporate job that promised financial stability and prestige. On the other was a lower-paying nonprofit role that resonated deeply with his passion for social impact. With student loans looming and societal expectations weighing heavily, Alex chose the corporate job, convincing himself it was the "responsible" decision.

At first, the allure of a steady paycheck and a bustling office filled Alex with excitement. But as months turned into years, a gnawing sense of dissatisfaction began to creep in. The work, while lucrative, felt hollow. The projects he dedicated himself to lacked the sense of purpose he had once envisioned for his career. Each day, Alex felt further removed from the idealistic graduate who had dreamed of making a difference.

One weekend, on a whim, Alex joined a local volunteering initiative organized by his company. It was a small gesture—a single Saturday spent helping to renovate a community center—but it awakened something within him. The joy and fulfillment he felt reminded him of what he truly valued. Inspired by that moment, Alex began making subtle but significant changes. He started dedicating his weekends to volunteering, building connections with like-minded individuals. He joined a community group focused on youth education, where he rediscovered his passion for helping others.

These small choices didn't require Alex to abandon his corporate job overnight. Instead, they added layers of meaning to his life. Over time, the energy and fulfillment he gained from these activities spilled into his work, making him more engaged and driven. Eventually, Alex found a way to bridge both worlds, taking on corporate social responsibility initiatives at his company and mentoring younger colleagues with a focus on purpose-driven leadership.

Takeaway: Alex's free will initially led him to prioritize financial stability, but life's balancing forces gently nudged him back toward his deeper purpose. His story shows that even within seemingly rigid choices, small actions can realign us with our values, restoring balance and infusing life with meaning. Sometimes, it's not about drastic leaps but steady steps toward the life that truly resonates with who you are.

Fate as the Protector of Balance

While free will allows you to make bold moves, fate steps in to prevent extremes, ensuring that your choices don't lead to chaos or imbalance. Setbacks, redirections, and even failures are fate's way of recalibrating your journey.

Example: Lisa's Perfectionism

Lisa had always been the epitome of excellence. A high-achieving professional, she prided herself on her relentless drive to deliver flawless results, whether it was at work, in her friendships, or even in her hobbies. To her, perfection wasn't just a goal—it was the standard. Her calendar was packed, her to-do lists meticulously detailed, and her reputation as the "go-to person" solidified.

But as the months wore on, cracks began to show. Late nights at the office became the norm, weekends were sacrificed for revisions no one else would have noticed, and her relationships began to strain under the weight of her constant busyness. Lisa told herself she could handle it—until one morning, she couldn't. She woke up feeling completely depleted, physically and emotionally. For the first time in her life, she had to step away from work, her body and mind demanding rest she could no longer deny.

In the quiet that followed, Lisa found herself face-to-face with her perfectionism. At first, it was uncomfortable; she replayed all the deadlines she'd missed, the emails unanswered, and the colleagues who had to pick up the slack. But as the days turned into weeks, Lisa began to reflect more deeply. Why had she set such impossible standards for herself? Why had she tied her worth so closely to her achievements?

Through therapy and intentional self-reflection, Lisa uncovered a new perspective. She realized that her pursuit of perfection had often come at the cost of her well-being and the connections she valued most. For the first time, she allowed herself to rest without guilt, to accept help without shame, and to embrace the idea that imperfection was not failure—it was humanity.

When Lisa eventually returned to work, she was different. She approached her projects with a balanced mindset, prioritizing collaboration and realistic goals over endless revisions. Her relationships, once strained, began to thrive as she made space for vulnerability and authenticity. Lisa's recalibration didn't mean abandoning her drive; it meant aligning it with self-care and compassion, creating a healthier version of success.

Takeaway: Lisa's burnout wasn't a punishment—it was life's way of recalibrating her path. It taught her that perfection isn't the pinnacle of achievement; balance is. By embracing imperfection and prioritizing her well-being, Lisa found a way to reconnect with her ambitions while honoring the person behind them. Sometimes, the most valuable growth comes from learning to let go.

The Paradox of Control: Dynamic Opposites

Free will and fate are often seen as opposites, but this framework reveals them as complementary forces working toward harmony. Each choice you make (free will) is met with a counterbalance (fate), creating a dynamic interplay that ensures your life remains aligned with your purpose.

Example: Thalia's Unexpected Detour

Thalia had always been a dreamer. From her university days as an architecture student, she imagined herself designing breathtaking skyscrapers for a prestigious firm, her name etched on iconic blueprints. Armed with her degree, an impressive portfolio, and unshakable determination, she set her sights on landing a position at one of the top firms in the city.

But reality didn't align with her ambitions. Rejection followed rejection, each email bearing the same polite yet crushing message: "Thank you for applying, but we've chosen another candidate." As weeks turned into months, Thalia's confidence wavered. Doubts crept in, whispering that maybe she wasn't as talented as she had believed.

Reluctantly, she accepted a position at a smaller firm—a far cry from her aspirations. At first, it felt like settling, a detour from the grand path she had envisioned. Her new office was modest, the projects humbler, and her colleagues fewer in number. But as Thalia adjusted, she began to notice something unexpected.

Unlike the rigid hierarchy she had anticipated at larger firms, the smaller company encouraged collaboration and creativity. Thalia was given the freedom to lead projects, experiment with bold designs, and even work closely with clients to bring their visions to life. These opportunities challenged her to develop her own style—one that combined functionality with artistry in a way that felt deeply personal and fulfilling.

The work wasn't glamorous, but it was meaningful. Over time, Thalia's projects gained recognition within the local community, and her confidence soared. She began to see that her initial rejections hadn't been failures—they had been redirections, guiding her toward an environment where she could grow and thrive in ways she hadn't imagined.

Years later, when Thalia was approached by a prestigious firm offering her a leadership role, she hesitated. Her smaller firm, once a compromise, had become a place where her creativity flourished, her voice mattered, and her values aligned. In the end, Thalia chose to stay, realizing that success wasn't about the size of the firm but the fulfillment she found in her work.

Takeaway: Fate doesn't dictate your life—it guides it, ensuring that even unexpected detours lead to meaningful destinations. Thalia's journey reminds us that the path we envision isn't always the one that will bring us the greatest growth or joy. Sometimes, the opportunities we never sought turn out to be the ones that shape us most profoundly.

Embracing the Balance

Understanding the interplay between free will and fate allows you to approach life with clarity and trust. Setbacks are not failures—they are recalibrations that guide you back to balance. Likewise, resistance isn't a sign of weakness but a nudge toward alignment.

Practical Strategies:

1. **Pause and Reflect**: When faced with challenges, take a step back and assess the situation. Ask yourself: Is life nudging me toward a different path?
2. **Recognize Patterns**: Reflect on past experiences where setbacks led to unexpected growth. These patterns reveal life's balancing forces at work.
3. **Stay Flexible**: Embrace redirection and remain open to new opportunities. Balance often emerges from adaptability.

Conclusion: Trust the Dance

Free will and fate are not adversaries—they're partners in a dynamic dance. Your choices shape your path, but fate ensures that your journey remains balanced and meaningful. By embracing this interplay, you can navigate life's challenges with resilience, clarity, and hope.

As we move into the next chapter, we'll explore how setbacks—often perceived as failures—are actually life's recalibration in action. Together, we'll learn to embrace these moments as opportunities for growth and alignment.

Chapter 05

Setbacks as Recalibration, Not Failure

Setbacks are among life's most challenging experiences. Whether it's a failed project, a lost relationship, or an unfulfilled dream, these moments can feel like crushing failures, leaving us frustrated, disheartened, and uncertain about the future. But what if setbacks weren't failures at all?

What if they were essential parts of life's recalibration process—a way of realigning you toward a path that ensures greater balance, growth, and fulfillment? In this chapter, we'll explore how setbacks fit into the dynamic balancing system of life, reframing them as opportunities for redirection and personal transformation.

Setbacks: The Scenic Detours of Life

Imagine you're driving toward a destination when you encounter a detour sign. At first, you feel annoyed—your planned route is disrupted, and you're forced to take a longer, unfamiliar path. But as you follow the detour, you notice scenic views you never would have seen otherwise. When you finally reach your destination, you realize the detour enriched your journey.

This is how setbacks often function. They may seem disruptive or unfair at the moment, but they guide you to experiences, opportunities, or lessons that contribute to your growth and alignment in ways your original plan never could.

The Purpose of Setbacks

Setbacks are life's way of recalibrating your path. They serve three essential purposes:

1. To Protect You from Extremes

When your choices or circumstances veer too far in one direction, setbacks restore balance.

Example: Overworking yourself to the point of burnout is life's way of signaling the need for rest and self-care.

2. To Teach Valuable Lessons

Every challenge offers insights, resilience, and personal growth.

Example: A failed business venture might teach you lessons about leadership, adaptability, and strategic thinking that set the stage for future success.

3. To Open Unexpected Doors

Setbacks often redirect you to opportunities you wouldn't have pursued otherwise.

Example: Missing out on one job might lead you to discover a role that better aligns with your skills and passions.

Example 1: A Career Detour

Rahul was the kind of software engineer who lived and breathed innovation. Ever since his university days, he dreamed of working at a prestigious tech company—a place where his skills could shine and his ideas could transform the industry. For months, he prepared meticulously, fine-tuning his resume, mastering coding challenges, and researching every detail about his dream employer.

When the rejection email arrived, it felt like the air had been knocked out of him. The words, polite but final, seemed to mock the hours of effort and hope he had poured into his application. Rahul spiraled into self-doubt, replaying every interview question and wondering if he was even good enough to succeed in his field.

Unable to dwell indefinitely, he decided to take the next best option—a position at a smaller, lesser-known company. It felt like settling for a consolation prize. On his first day, as he stepped into the modest office, Rahul resolved to treat it as a temporary stop, a placeholder until he could apply again to the big leagues.

But as weeks turned into months, something surprising happened. The smaller company, with its lean teams and hands-on approach, allowed Rahul to dive into projects he never would have touched as a junior at a prestigious firm. He found himself leading a team to develop cutting-edge technology, making decisions that had a real impact, and learning skills far beyond coding—like leadership, project management, and client communication.

His confidence began to rebuild. The sense of ownership he felt over his work reignited his passion for innovation. Rahul realized that the rejection he had once viewed as a failure had led him to an environment where he could grow not just as an engineer, but as a leader.

Two years later, with a wealth of experience under his belt, Rahul reapplied to his dream company. This time, the interviews felt different—he wasn't just answering questions; he was sharing stories of challenges overcome, systems built from scratch, and teams led to success. When the offer letter finally came through, it wasn't just validation of his skills—it was proof that the detour had been an integral part of his journey.

Takeaway: Rahul's setback wasn't a failure—it was life recalibrating his path to allow for greater growth and alignment. Sometimes, the paths that feel like compromises lead us to opportunities that prepare us for the dreams we're destined to achieve.

Example 2: The End of a Relationship

Sofia and Daniel were the kind of couple everyone thought would make it. High school sweethearts with dreams of a shared future, they planned everything together—college, careers, marriage, and even the names of their future children. Their love was the foundation of Sofia's world, giving her a sense of stability and purpose. But as they entered adulthood, their paths began to diverge. Daniel's corporate ambitions demanded long hours and constant travel, while Sofia felt drawn to creative teaching opportunities and volunteering in underserved communities. Slowly, they realized they wanted different things.

The day Daniel ended their relationship, Sofia's world crumbled. Sitting across from her in their favorite café, he broke the news with trembling hands. "I don't think we're heading in the same direction anymore," he said, his eyes filled with regret. For Sofia, it felt like her future had been erased. She couldn't imagine life without him—his laugh, his support, the dreams they had built together. In the days that followed, every memory felt like a sharp knife, cutting deeper into her grief.

The pain became unbearable. Sofia withdrew from her friends, her family, and even her job. Every corner of her apartment reminded her of the life she thought they would share. One night, overcome by hopelessness, Sofia made a desperate attempt to end her suffering. She swallowed a handful of pills, convinced there was no way forward. But fate stepped in—her sister, sensing something was wrong, came by unannounced and found her in time to rush her to the hospital.

Waking up in a sterile hospital room, Sofia felt an overwhelming mix of shame, despair, and an unfamiliar flicker of relief. As her sister held her hand, tears streaming down her face, Sofia realized she had been given a second chance. The road ahead wasn't clear, but for the first time, she felt the faintest glimmer of hope.

Healing wasn't immediate, nor was it easy. Therapy became her anchor, helping her confront the depth of her pain and begin the process of rebuilding her life. Slowly, she started reclaiming pieces of herself. She enrolled in a master's program in education, channeling her energy into a passion she had always set aside. She traveled to new places, finding inspiration in the beauty of different cultures and the resilience of the people she met. And through volunteering at a local school, she rediscovered a sense of purpose and joy she hadn't felt in years.

It was during one of her teaching assignments abroad that Sofia met Marco, a fellow educator with a heart for service. They bonded over late-night conversations about their dreams and shared values. Unlike her relationship with Daniel, her connection with Marco felt different—rooted in mutual respect, understanding, and the alignment of their aspirations. For the first time in a long while, Sofia felt like she was building a future with someone who truly saw and supported her.

Years later, Sofia could look back on her breakup with Daniel with a sense of peace. The pain had been real and consuming, but it had also been the catalyst for her transformation. Losing Daniel had forced her to confront herself, to grow in ways she hadn't thought possible, and to build a life that reflected her truest self. Marco wasn't a replacement for Daniel—he was the partner she was meant to find after discovering who she was on her own.

Takeaway: Sofia's loss wasn't the end of her story; it was a recalibration that allowed her to evolve, align with her values, and ultimately find a love that complemented the life she had built. Her journey reminds us that even the darkest moments can pave the way for growth, purpose, and unexpected joy.

Practical Tools for Navigating Setbacks

To embrace setbacks as opportunities for recalibration, you need a shift in perspective and practical strategies. Here's how to start:

1. Reframe the Narrative

Instead of viewing setbacks as failures, see them as part of life's balancing process.

Exercise: Write down three challenges you've faced in the past. Reflect on the lessons or opportunities they brought. This exercise helps you recognize how setbacks have served your growth.

2. Focus on the Long-Term View

Remember that life's balance unfolds over time. Setbacks are often the seeds of future growth.

Example: A tree in winter appears dormant, but beneath the surface, it's gathering energy for spring. Your setback is like winter—preparing you for a season of renewal.

3. Trust the Process

Have faith that life's balancing forces are working in your favor, even when the outcome isn't immediately clear.

Affirmation: Repeat to yourself: *"This is not the end of my story. Life is recalibrating me for something better."*

4. Stay Open to New Opportunities

Setbacks often open doors to paths you hadn't considered. Stay curious and willing to explore unexpected possibilities.

Example: If a job falls through, consider freelancing, volunteering, or pursuing a passion project. These detours often lead to surprising opportunities.

5. Practice Gratitude

Gratitude shifts your focus from what you've lost to what you still have. This mindset helps you see setbacks as part of a larger picture.

Exercise: Write down three things you're grateful for each day. Over time, this practice builds resilience and optimism.

Setbacks and Growth: The Bigger Picture

Setbacks are not punishments—they are recalibrations that guide you toward greater alignment and fulfillment. When viewed through the lens of balance, setbacks reveal their true value:

- **They Build Resilience**: Challenges strengthen your ability to adapt and persevere.
- **They Encourage Self-Discovery**: Setbacks often reveal hidden strengths or passions.
- **They Realign You with Your Purpose**: By redirecting you, setbacks ensure your path aligns with your values and long-term goals.

Example 3: A Personal Transformation

David had always defined himself by his career. A middle-aged professional who had spent decades climbing the corporate ladder, he prided himself on his work ethic and achievements. His corner office, frequent business trips, and accolades were not just symbols of success—they were the foundation of his identity. But when his company underwent a sudden restructuring, David found himself staring at a severance letter. The layoff wasn't personal, his manager assured him, but the words felt hollow. To David, it wasn't just a job he had lost; it was a part of who he was.

In the weeks that followed, David struggled to make sense of his new reality. Mornings felt aimless without the buzz of emails and meetings, and he avoided running into former colleagues, embarrassed to admit he was no longer "successful" in the way he had once been. The silence of his days was deafening, amplifying his feelings of failure and loss. At night, he would sit in his study, staring at the framed awards on the wall, questioning whether all those years of hard work had been for nothing.

One afternoon, while sorting through old files, David came across a thank-you letter from a junior colleague he had mentored years ago. The letter spoke of how David's guidance had shaped the young man's career and inspired him to take bold steps toward his goals. The words struck a chord in David, awakening a memory of how much he had enjoyed mentoring others, even amidst the grind of corporate life.

Tentatively, David began exploring this forgotten passion. It wasn't easy at first—reaching out to local business networks and offering to mentor young entrepreneurs felt daunting. What if no one valued his experience? But he pushed past his doubts, and the response he received was overwhelmingly positive. At first, it was just a way to pass the time, but soon, he found himself deeply engaged. Helping others navigate challenges and find their footing reignited something within him—a sense of purpose he hadn't felt in years. His mentees appreciated his wisdom, and their successes became a source of pride and fulfillment.

Encouraged by their feedback, David decided to take things further. Drawing on his decades of experience, he launched his own consultancy. The venture allowed him to work on his own terms, focusing on projects he was passionate about while maintaining a flexible schedule that gave him time to rediscover hobbies and reconnect with his family. For the first time in years, David felt a balance he had never thought possible during his corporate climb.

Looking back, David realized that being laid off wasn't the end of his career—it was a turning point. The job he had clung to had defined him, but it had also limited him. Losing it forced him to reevaluate his priorities and rediscover his passions, ultimately leading to a life that felt more aligned with his values and aspirations.

Takeaway: David's layoff wasn't a failure—it was life's way of recalibrating his path, allowing him to build resilience, rediscover his purpose, and realign his life with his values. His journey reminds us that even the most unsettling changes can be opportunities for transformation, growth, and fulfillment. Sometimes, what feels like an ending is just the beginning of something greater.

Moving Forward

When life throws you a curveball, remember: setbacks are not dead ends. They are detours guiding you toward a better path. By trusting the process, staying open to opportunities, and embracing growth, you can transform obstacles into stepping stones.

Looking Ahead

In the next chapter, we'll explore how comparison disrupts balance and fuels frustration. You'll learn why trusting your unique journey is essential for contentment and how to let go of envy to focus on the harmony that makes your life uniquely meaningful.

Chapter 06

Letting Go of Comparison

Comparison is often called the thief of joy—and for good reason. When we measure our lives against others, it's easy to feel inadequate, envious, or frustrated. Yet, as we've explored in this framework, each person's life operates within its own unique balancing system. Comparing your journey to someone else's is like comparing apples to oranges—or an actively traded stock to a dormant one. Both follow their own rules and rhythms, and judging one by the other's standards leads to unnecessary dissatisfaction.

In this chapter, we'll delve into why comparison is so tempting yet misleading, how it disrupts your sense of balance, and practical ways to embrace your unique path. By the end, you'll have the tools to release comparison and focus on the beauty of your own journey.

Why Comparison Feels So Natural

As social beings, humans are wired to observe and evaluate others. This instinct, rooted in survival, once helped our ancestors learn from others' successes and failures. However, in today's hyperconnected world, where social media presents curated versions of people's lives, this instinct often backfires.

Example: The Social Media Trap

Maya, a devoted working mother, often ended her long, exhausting days by sinking into the couch with her phone. Social media had become her escape, a brief reprieve from the chaos of managing work deadlines, household chores, and caring for her two young children. But as she scrolled through her feed one evening, the sense of escape turned into a sinking feeling.

One post showed a college friend basking in the golden glow of a Maldives sunset, her caption filled with hashtags about luxury and gratitude. Another post featured a former coworker celebrating a big promotion, her smile radiant as she clinked glasses in a sleek corporate office. A third was from an acquaintance flaunting a sparkling engagement ring, surrounded by congratulatory comments. Maya's heart sank. She glanced around her living room, where toys were scattered, dishes were piled in the sink, and the faint hum of work emails buzzed in her mind. Compared to their glamorous, successful lives, hers felt mundane and inadequate.

What Maya didn't see—and what those posts didn't show—were the realities behind the pictures. The friend in the Maldives was drowning in debt, financing her dream vacation with a credit card she couldn't pay off. The newly promoted coworker was overwhelmed by her workload and silently questioning whether the raise was worth the stress. The beaming couple with the engagement ring had recently been through a major argument, their relationship far from the picture-perfect image they portrayed online.

Yet, in that moment, Maya wasn't thinking about these hidden struggles. She was trapped in the illusion that everyone else had it together while she barely managed to hold on. Her scrolling turned into spiraling—she questioned her choices, her achievements, and even her worth. "Why can't I have what they have?" she wondered, as tears blurred her vision.

It wasn't until Maya spoke to a close friend that she began to understand the impact of these curated comparisons. Her friend, who had also wrestled with similar feelings, reminded her that social media was just a highlight reel, not a full story. Slowly, Maya started shifting her focus. Instead of scrolling mindlessly, she began setting boundaries around her social media use. She filled her evenings with journaling, connecting with her family, and reflecting on her own victories—like the time she landed a big project at work, or the handmade birthday cake her daughter had loved.

Over time, Maya realized her life wasn't lacking—it was uniquely hers, full of quiet triumphs and moments of love that no filter could capture.

Takeaway: Comparison often thrives on incomplete information, creating a distorted perception of others' lives and unfair judgments of your own. Social media may highlight the peaks, but it obscures the valleys, leaving out the struggles and imperfections that make us human. Maya's journey reminds us to step back, refocus on our own path, and celebrate the richness of the lives we live beyond the screen.

The Stock Market Analogy: Comparing Apples to Oranges

As we've discussed earlier, actively traded stocks (balanced lives) and dormant stocks (unbalanced lives) operate differently. Comparing them is not only unproductive—it's inherently misleading.

Actively Traded Stocks: Balanced Lives

- These lives experience frequent adjustments, ensuring that challenges and successes align with their unique paths.
- They may lack dramatic highs, but their steady recalibration leads to long-term fulfillment and stability.

Dormant Stocks: Unbalanced Lives

- These lives may experience extreme highs (sudden promotions, unexpected windfalls) or lows (drastic failures, instability).

- Their apparent success may be temporary, as imbalances often lead to sudden corrections.

Example: A Tale of Two Colleagues

Jake and Ethan started their careers at the same company, but their approaches to work couldn't have been more different. Jake, methodical and consistent, believed in steady progress. He approached his tasks with care, took on additional training to expand his skill set, and built strong relationships with his colleagues. Each year, his efforts were rewarded with modest but steady raises, a reflection of his dependable growth.

Ethan, on the other hand, was a whirlwind of charm and confidence. While Jake stayed late to refine his reports or learn new software, Ethan focused on visibility. He spent time networking with senior management, attending every company event, and taking credit for team successes. His charisma paid off, and within a year, Ethan had landed a coveted promotion that left Jake feeling a pang of envy. How had Ethan, who seemed to breeze through tasks with minimal effort, leapt ahead so quickly?

But the story didn't end there. Ethan's new role brought increased responsibilities—complex projects, tight deadlines, and leadership demands he hadn't anticipated. Without the foundation of skills and experience Jake had been quietly building, Ethan struggled to meet expectations. Mistakes piled up, and the cracks in his once-seamless performance began to show. Meanwhile, Jake's steady progress was noticed by his supervisors. When a senior position became available two years later, Jake's track record made him the obvious choice.

The contrast between their journeys became clear. Ethan's early success had been impressive but fleeting, built on a foundation that couldn't sustain the weight of long-term challenges. Jake's approach, though slower, provided the resilience and readiness to seize larger opportunities when the time was right.

Takeaway: Comparing Jake's balanced, steady growth to Ethan's meteoric rise highlights the dangers of judging paths too quickly. Ethan's temporary highs were unsustainable, while Jake's consistent recalibration ensured long-term success. Life, much like Jake's journey, rewards those who build with patience and purpose.

How Comparison Disrupts Balance

Comparison doesn't just distract you—it actively disrupts your sense of balance. Here's how:

1. It Distracts from Your Path

Constantly focusing on others pulls your attention away from your unique journey, making it harder to appreciate your progress.

2. It Breeds Dissatisfaction

Envy magnifies what you lack while minimizing what you already have, creating a distorted and negative view of your life.

3. It Undermines Contentment

True contentment comes from aligning with your own balance—not meeting someone else's external benchmarks.

Practical Strategies to Let Go of Comparison

1. Reframe Your Perspective

- Instead of seeing others' success as a threat, view it as evidence of what's possible.
- **Exercise**: Write down three qualities or achievements you admire in someone else. Then reflect on how these qualities can inspire your own growth.

2. Focus on Gratitude

- Gratitude shifts your focus from what's missing to what you have.
- **Exercise**: At the end of each day, list three things you're grateful for. Over time, this practice cultivates a mindset of appreciation.

3. Embrace Your Unique Journey

- Remind yourself that your life is governed by its own balancing system. What works for someone else may not align with your purpose.
- **Affirmation**: Repeat to yourself: *"I trust my journey and its balance. My path is mine alone."*

4. Limit Social Media

- Social media often amplifies comparison. If it's a trigger for envy, consider taking breaks or curating your feed to include content that uplifts and inspires you.
- **Example**: Maya replaced her evening social media scrolling with a gratitude journal. This small shift transformed her perspective and brought her greater peace.

5. Celebrate Small Wins

- Focus on the small steps you're taking toward your goals. These steps contribute to your life's balance and growth.
- **Exercise**: Create a "win list" where you document small achievements each week. Over time, this list becomes a powerful reminder of your progress.

Comparison as a Tool for Growth

Rather than viewing comparison as a threat, use it as a tool for self-reflection. When you feel envy or dissatisfaction, ask yourself:

- *What does this feeling reveal about my own goals and values?*

- *How can I use this observation to inspire growth without undermining my contentment?*

Example: Turning Envy into Action

Lena couldn't help but feel a twinge of envy whenever she saw her friend Clara's social media posts. Clara always seemed to have a new project to share—a pottery workshop one week, a photography exhibition the next. Her life seemed brimming with creativity and fulfillment, and every new post left Lena questioning her own choices. Why didn't she have a passion like that? Why did her days feel so routine?

At first, Lena's envy was paralyzing. She scrolled through Clara's posts with a mixture of admiration and self-doubt, wondering if she was simply too late to discover her own creative spark. But one evening, as she put her phone down, Lena decided to shift her perspective. Instead of seeing Clara's hobbies as a source of comparison, she began to view them as inspiration. What was it about Clara's life that resonated so deeply with her? It wasn't the specific activities—it was Clara's curiosity and willingness to explore.

With that realization, Lena made a decision. The next day, she signed up for a local painting class—a medium she had dabbled in years ago but abandoned amidst the busyness of work and life. Walking into the studio that first evening, Lena felt a nervous excitement. The scent of paints, the blank canvas in front of her, the guidance of the instructor—all of it felt like a world she had been missing. Week by week, her confidence grew, and so did her sense of fulfillment. What started as a simple act of curiosity blossomed into a rekindled passion.

Over time, Lena found herself smiling as she scrolled through Clara's posts—not with envy, but with a sense of camaraderie. She even shared her own creations, joining the vibrant circle of creativity she once envied.

Takeaway: Lena's story shows how envy, when approached mindfully, can be a gateway to growth. By shifting her perspective and taking action, she transformed comparison into a catalyst for rediscovery, proving that inspiration often lies within what we admire most in others.

Trusting Your Unique Balance

The core lesson of this framework is that each life operates within its own system of balance. Trusting this balance means letting go of external benchmarks and focusing on what feels right for you. Others' paths may seem more successful or fulfilling, but their journeys are governed by entirely different dynamics.

Your life's unique balance ensures you're exactly where you're meant to be.

Looking Ahead

In the next chapter, we'll explore how to rebuild balance after major setbacks, such as loss or grief. You'll learn to trust the process even in life's darkest moments and discover tools for finding purpose and peace in the aftermath of adversity.

Chapter 07

Rebuilding Balance After Loss or Grief

Loss is one of life's most profound challenges. Whether it's the death of a loved one, the end of a relationship, or the collapse of a cherished dream, these moments can leave us feeling untethered—as though life's balance has been shattered beyond repair. Yet, as we've seen in this framework, loss, like setbacks, is part of life's dynamic recalibration process. While the pain is real and raw, it is also a temporary imbalance—a phase that opens the door to growth, transformation, and renewed meaning.

In this chapter, we'll explore how to rebuild balance after loss. Through real-life examples and practical strategies, you'll learn how to trust life's recalibration process, navigate grief, and eventually find peace and purpose.

Loss as a Temporary Imbalance

Loss disrupts our equilibrium because it removes something—or someone—integral to our identity. This absence creates a void that feels insurmountable. However, this void is not permanent. Over time, life introduces new elements—relationships, passions, and opportunities—that gradually restore balance, albeit in a transformed way.

The Analogy of the Broken Scale

Imagine your life as a perfectly balanced scale. When loss occurs, it's as though one side of the scale has been removed entirely, causing the other side to crash to the ground. At first, the imbalance feels overwhelming. But as new elements are added, the scale begins to stabilize. While it may never look exactly as it did before, it can achieve a new, meaningful equilibrium.

Example: Lila's Loss

Lila's world shattered when she lost her husband of 30 years to a sudden illness. He had been her partner in everything—her confidant, her rock, and the love of her life. In the months that followed, Lila felt an unbearable void, as though the rhythm of her life had abruptly stopped. The mornings were the hardest. She would wake up, instinctively reach for the other side of the bed, and find only emptiness. Her once-joyful routines, like sharing coffee on the porch or planning their next trip, became painful reminders of what she had lost.

Lila found herself retreating from the world, unsure of how to navigate this new reality. But over time, she decided to take small, brave steps forward. She joined a grief support group, though at first, she wasn't sure if she could share her pain with strangers. To her surprise, she found kindred spirits—people who understood her sorrow without needing explanations. Through their stories and support, she began to feel less alone.

One day, while going through a box of her husband's belongings, Lila found a notebook filled with sketches and plans for a garden they had dreamed of creating together. Inspired, she decided to honor his memory by bringing that dream to life. At first, it was a way to keep him close, a connection to the love they had shared. But as the seasons passed, the garden grew into more than a tribute. It became a source of healing, a place where she could channel her grief into something beautiful and life-giving.

Every flower she planted, every weed she pulled, felt like a conversation with him, a way to keep his presence alive. Her garden became her sanctuary, a living testament to their love and her own resilience—a reminder that even in the face of profound loss, life can bloom again.

Takeaway: Lila's grief was a temporary imbalance. By engaging with life, she allowed new elements to restore her equilibrium, honoring her loss while embracing growth.

Grief and the Balancing Process

Grief is not something you "get over." It becomes part of your story, shaping you in profound ways. Life's balancing forces don't erase the loss—they help you coexist with it, eventually finding a way to move forward.

Principle 1: Grief Takes Time

- Emotional balance is a gradual process, unfolding over time.
- **Practical Tip**: Be patient with yourself. Healing is not linear, and setbacks are a natural part of the process.

Principle 2: Growth Emerges from Loss

- Loss creates space for new opportunities, relationships, or perspectives that weren't possible before.

Example: Bella had spent over a decade climbing the corporate ladder at a prestigious marketing agency. She loved the structure, the routine, and the camaraderie of her team. But when her company underwent a sudden restructuring, Bella found herself holding a pink slip instead of the promotion she had anticipated. The loss was devastating. Overnight, her carefully crafted identity as a career-driven professional crumbled.

For weeks, Bella grappled with a sense of purposelessness. Mornings that had once been a whirlwind of meetings and deadlines now stretched out in silence. At first, she threw herself into job applications, desperate to replicate the life she had lost. But rejection after rejection left her even more disheartened.

One day, while organizing old files on her computer, Bella stumbled upon a folder filled with essays and short stories she had written years ago as a hobby. As she read through them, she felt a flicker of something she hadn't experienced in weeks—joy. On impulse, she decided to post one of her essays on a blogging platform. The positive feedback she received was overwhelming, with readers connecting to her words and asking for more.

Encouraged, Bella started writing regularly—short pieces on personal growth, resilience, and navigating uncertainty. Writing became her sanctuary, a way to process her emotions and rediscover her voice. One of her blog posts caught the attention of a local magazine editor, who offered her a chance to contribute as a freelance writer.

What began as a therapeutic outlet soon transformed into a new career path. Bella embraced freelance writing, enjoying the freedom to choose projects that resonated with her passions. She found herself collaborating with nonprofits, writing heartfelt pieces about their causes, and even ghostwriting memoirs for clients. For the first time, Bella felt truly aligned with her work, free from the rigid constraints of her corporate job.

As Bella's portfolio grew, so did her confidence. She reflected on how losing her job—an event she had once seen as a failure—had created the space for her to uncover her true calling. Freelance writing allowed her to explore her creative side, set her own schedule, and find a work-life balance that she had never imagined possible.

Lesson:

Bella's story illustrates how loss, while painful, can pave the way for growth and transformation. By embracing the opportunity to explore her passions, Bella turned a moment of uncertainty into a chapter of fulfillment and purpose. Her journey reminds us that when one door closes, it often creates the space needed to discover new and unexpected possibilities.

Principle 3: Balance Looks Different After Loss

- Life's balance doesn't mean returning to "normal." It means finding a new equilibrium that honors the loss while embracing what lies ahead.

Example: John's world was shattered when his wife, Margaret, passed away after 40 years of marriage. She had been his partner, confidant, and best friend—a constant presence in every corner of his life. Their home, once filled with the warmth of shared laughter and quiet companionship, now felt achingly empty.

In the months following her passing, John found himself drifting through his days. Simple tasks like making breakfast or sitting in the garden they had tended together brought back a flood of memories that left him immobilized. He was stuck between holding onto the life they had built together and grappling with the overwhelming void her absence left behind.

At first, John resisted invitations to reengage with his community, retreating instead into his grief. But one Sunday morning, feeling restless, he decided to attend his local church—an activity he and Margaret had once cherished together. After the service, a young couple approached him. They had recently gotten married and were struggling to navigate the challenges of building a life together. Seeing John's kind demeanor and wisdom, they asked if he had any advice.

The conversation sparked something in John. He shared stories of his own marriage—how he and Margaret had faced disagreements, weathered hardships, and grown closer through the years. The couple listened intently, their gratitude evident. For the first time in months, John felt a sense of purpose.

Encouraged by the experience, John began volunteering at the church's mentorship program for young couples. What started as a small commitment quickly grew into something deeply meaningful. John became a trusted guide for couples navigating the complexities of relationships, sharing his experiences with honesty and compassion. Through his stories, he felt Margaret's presence—not as a painful reminder of what he had lost, but as a legacy of love that he could pass on to others.

Over time, John's grief transformed. While the ache of missing Margaret never fully disappeared, it became interwoven with a sense of gratitude for the life they had shared and the wisdom their relationship had given him. His role as a mentor gave him a new equilibrium—a way to honor his loss while embracing the connections and purpose that lay ahead.

Lesson:

John's story illustrates that balance after loss doesn't mean returning to the life you once knew. It's about finding a new equilibrium that acknowledges the pain of what's gone while creating space for meaningful growth and connection. By channeling his grief into mentorship, John discovered a renewed sense of purpose and a way to keep Margaret's memory alive. His journey reminds us that even in the aftermath of profound loss, there is the potential to rebuild and find meaning in the next chapter.

Navigating Loss: Practical Strategies

1. Acknowledge Your Pain

- **Why It Matters**: Ignoring grief only prolongs imbalance. Acknowledging your emotions is the first step toward healing.
- **Exercise**: Write a letter to what or whom you've lost, expressing your feelings honestly. This practice helps process emotions and begin to release them.

2. Trust the Process

- **Why It Matters**: Loss feels overwhelming because the future seems uncertain. Trusting life's balancing process can bring comfort, reminding you that new opportunities will emerge.
- **Affirmation**: Repeat to yourself: "This pain is part of my recalibration. I trust that life will restore balance in time."

3. Stay Open to New Connections

- Why It Matters: Loss can leave you feeling isolated, but engaging with others helps rebuild balance.

Example: Quentin's life took an unexpected turn when his longtime partner, Aaron, passed away after a sudden illness. Their home, once a haven of shared dreams and laughter, now felt heavy with silence. Quentin, a naturally introverted person, found himself withdrawing even further, avoiding friends and family. The thought of sharing his pain or explaining his grief felt exhausting.

Months passed, and Quentin's isolation deepened. Simple joys like cooking—a passion he had shared with Aaron—became unbearable reminders of what he had lost. His days blurred together in a cycle of work and solitude, and he began to question if he could ever find meaning in life again.

One evening, at the gentle urging of his sister, Quentin reluctantly agreed to attend a grief support group at a nearby community center. Walking into the room filled with strangers sharing their own stories of loss was overwhelming at first. He felt out of place and unsure of whether he could open up. But as the weeks went by, Quentin started to share snippets of his story. To his surprise, the group didn't pity him—they simply listened, nodding in understanding. For the first time, Quentin felt seen and less alone in his grief.

Encouraged by the support group's warmth, Quentin decided to take another step. He signed up to volunteer at a local LGBTQ+ community center, a cause close to Aaron's heart. At first, the work was daunting, but over time, Quentin found joy in organizing events, mentoring young members of the community, and creating spaces where others could feel safe and connected.

Through these new connections, Quentin began to heal. He forged friendships with people who admired his resilience and kindness, and their presence filled some of the void left by Aaron's absence. Slowly, Quentin rediscovered his love for cooking, hosting small gatherings where he shared his culinary creations with his newfound friends.

These interactions didn't erase Quentin's grief, but they gave him a renewed sense of purpose and connection. He realized that while Aaron's loss would always be a part of his story, it didn't have to define his future. By opening himself to new relationships and experiences, Quentin found a way to honor Aaron's memory while embracing the possibilities of life ahead.

Lesson:

Quentin's journey highlights the importance of staying open to new connections, even when grief feels all-consuming. By stepping outside his comfort zone and engaging with others, he discovered sources of healing and meaning that helped rebuild his sense of balance. His story reminds us that isolation, while tempting in the face of loss, often deepens the pain. Connection—whether through support groups, volunteering, or rekindling old friendships—can be a powerful catalyst for growth and renewal.

4. Find Purpose in Your Loss

- **Why It Matters**: Transforming grief into purpose integrates loss into your life story in a meaningful way.
- **Example**: Consider activities that honor your loss, such as creating a memorial, starting a scholarship fund, or dedicating time to a cause your loved one cared about.

5. Focus on Small Wins

- **Why It Matters**: Rebuilding balance after loss can feel overwhelming, but small steps create momentum.
- **Exercise**: Each day, identify one positive action you can take, whether it's going for a walk, calling a friend, or pursuing a hobby.

Example: David's Journey Through Grief

David's world shattered the day he lost his teenage son, Alex, in a tragic car accident. Alex had been the light of his life—his laughter filled their home, and his dreams for the future were as boundless as the sky. When the police knocked on his door with the devastating news, it felt as though time stopped. The weeks that followed were a blur of tears, silence, and an unbearable emptiness that consumed every corner of David's existence.

Grief paralyzed him. Simple tasks like getting out of bed felt insurmountable. He replayed the "what ifs" in his mind endlessly— what if Alex had taken a different route? What if he'd been there to stop him from going out that night? These thoughts spiraled into an abyss of guilt and despair. David withdrew from his friends, his work, and the world, convinced he would never again feel joy or purpose.

It was months later, at the gentle insistence of a friend, that David hesitantly attended a workshop for parents who had lost children. He didn't expect much, unsure if anything could ease the weight on his heart. But as he sat in the circle, listening to stories of heartbreak, survival, and resilience, something shifted within him. He saw in others what he thought he had lost forever—a spark of hope amidst the pain. They had been where he was, and yet, somehow, they had found ways to carry their grief and move forward.

Inspired by their strength, David began to look for ways to channel his sorrow into something meaningful. He started volunteering with a local road safety organization, sharing Alex's story in schools to raise awareness about safe driving. Each time he spoke, he felt a flicker of Alex's spirit alive in the mission. Encouraged by the impact he was making, David eventually founded a nonprofit dedicated to promoting safe driving for teens. The organization became a lifeline for him—a way to honor Alex's memory while potentially saving other families from experiencing the same pain.

David's journey didn't erase the grief, but it transformed it. Through his actions, he found a new balance—a way to carry Alex's legacy forward while rediscovering his own purpose. The laughter in his home didn't return in the same way, but the joy of helping others brought a new kind of light into his life.

Takeaway: David's loss was devastating, but his story reminds us that even the deepest pain can be a catalyst for purpose. By channeling his grief into action, David found a way to honor his son's memory and create a positive impact, showing that healing doesn't mean forgetting— it means building something meaningful in the space where loss resides.

When Loss Feels Overwhelming

Some losses feel so immense that finding balance again seems impossible. In these moments, it's essential to:

1. **Seek Professional Support**: Therapy or counseling can provide tools and guidance to navigate deep grief.
2. **Lean on Your Community**: Surround yourself with people who offer support and understanding.
3. **Give Yourself Time**: Healing doesn't have a timeline. Allow yourself to grieve at your own pace.

Finding Hope After Loss

Loss changes you, but it doesn't define you. By trusting life's balancing process, you can find hope, purpose, and even joy again. Your loss becomes part of your story—not the end, but a chapter that shapes what comes next.

Exercise: Reflecting on Balance After Loss

- Write about a previous loss you've experienced. What did it teach you? How did it shape your life?
- Reflect on how this perspective might apply to your current challenges.

Looking Ahead

Loss and grief are among the most profound imbalances we face, and rebuilding balance in their aftermath requires patience, resilience, and intentional effort. As we've explored in this chapter, healing begins with small steps, a willingness to embrace new connections, and the courage to honor both what was lost and what lies ahead.

But what about those who find themselves in the grip of even more extreme challenges—trauma, systemic barriers, or prolonged adversity? How can the principles of balance guide us in the face of overwhelming odds?

In the next chapter, we'll delve deeper into navigating these extreme scenarios. You'll discover how to create stability amidst chaos, find purpose in adversity, and take small yet transformative steps toward reclaiming equilibrium. Through relatable stories and actionable strategies, we'll explore how life's recalibration process remains a source of hope, even in the darkest moments.

When balance feels out of reach, trust that even the smallest efforts can spark a path forward. Let's uncover how to rebuild and thrive, no matter how insurmountable the challenge may seem.

Finding Balance in the Face of Extreme Challenges

Life is unpredictable, and while we strive for balance, extreme challenges—be they severe trauma, systemic barriers, or prolonged adversity—can upend our equilibrium entirely. In these moments, it's easy to feel trapped in a cycle of despair, as though the forces of life's recalibration have abandoned us. Yet even in the most difficult circumstances, the seeds of balance remain, waiting for us to nurture them.

In this chapter, we explore how to navigate these profound challenges, highlighting the importance of small, intentional steps, resilience, and the power of community and purpose.

Understanding the Nature of Extreme Imbalances

Unlike ordinary setbacks, extreme challenges can feel all-encompassing, leaving us without clear direction or hope. It's as though life's scale has been tipped so drastically that it feels impossible to restore balance. However, even in the most difficult situations, life seeks equilibrium.

The forest fire analogy is a useful way to understand this:

After a devastating forest fire, the landscape seems irreparably scarred. But beneath the ash, the roots of trees remain alive, and over time, new growth begins to emerge. Extreme challenges can feel like a fire that has consumed everything, but with patience and care, regrowth is possible.

Example: Asha's Escape from a War Zone

Asha's life was torn apart when a brutal conflict forced her to flee her home country. The once-vivid streets of her childhood, the laughter of family gatherings, and the comforting routines of daily life were replaced by chaos and uncertainty. With nothing but a small backpack and the haunting memories of what she had lost, Asha sought refuge in a foreign land—a place where she didn't speak the language, didn't know a soul, and felt like a stranger even to herself.

The early months were the hardest. The trauma of war followed her like a shadow. Flashbacks of the violence she had witnessed jolted her awake at night, leaving her exhausted and frightened. Simple tasks, like navigating the unfamiliar streets or buying groceries, felt insurmountable. The weight of displacement—of being uprooted from everything familiar—was a constant ache. Asha often found herself wondering if she would ever feel whole again.

For a time, she lived in survival mode, unsure of how to move forward. But life has a way of offering glimmers of hope, even in the darkest moments. One day, a kind neighbor knocked on her door, offering a plate of food and a warm smile. Though they didn't share a common language, the gesture broke through Asha's isolation. This neighbor became her first lifeline, patiently teaching her basic phrases in the local language. Slowly, Asha began to find her voice in this new world.

Encouraged by this small connection, she ventured out to a nearby community center that offered free classes for refugees. The center became her sanctuary—a place where she could learn, connect with others who understood her struggles, and begin to feel part of a community. Sharing her story with others who had faced similar hardships brought an unexpected comfort. She was no longer alone in her pain; she was part of a tapestry of resilience.

As Asha settled into this new routine, she found work as a caretaker for an elderly couple. The job gave her purpose and a steady income, allowing her to send money back to her family still affected by the war. But something deeper began to unfold when she joined an art therapy group at the community center. At first, she hesitated to pick up a brush, unsure if she could express the turmoil within her. But as the colors began to flow across the canvas, so did her emotions. Each stroke became a release, a way to process her grief and reclaim her story.

Her paintings, raw and vivid, resonated with others in her community. They spoke of loss, but also of hope—a delicate light shining through the cracks of despair. Word spread, and soon, Asha was invited to showcase her work at local events. She found herself standing in front of strangers, sharing the journey behind her art. Her voice, once silenced by war, became a beacon of resilience and courage.

Over time, Asha's paintings and speeches transformed her from a survivor to an advocate. Her art inspired others to confront their own pain, and her story became a testament to the strength of the human spirit. Through connection, creativity, and a willingness to take small, brave steps forward, Asha rebuilt a life that honored her past while embracing the possibilities of her future.

Takeaway:

Asha's journey illustrates the power of resilience and the profound impact of small acts of connection. By accepting support and embracing opportunities for growth, she transformed unimaginable loss into a renewed sense of purpose. Her story reminds us that even in the face of profound displacement and trauma, the human spirit can find ways to heal, thrive, and inspire others.

Principles for Navigating Extreme Challenges

Principle 1: Stability Before Balance

In extreme situations, survival often takes precedence over balance. Establishing stability—a safe environment, access to basic needs, and a support network—is the first step.

Practical Tip:

Focus on immediate needs. Seek out resources such as shelters, food banks, support groups, or local charities that can provide stability during difficult times.

Principle 2: Connection is a Lifeline

Isolation amplifies pain. Reaching out to others—whether friends, family, or support groups—can provide comfort, understanding, and practical help.

Example:

Luna's world changed in an instant when a devastating flood swept through her town, leaving behind a trail of destruction. Her home, once a place of warmth and laughter, was reduced to waterlogged ruins. Precious keepsakes—family photos, heirlooms, and mementos of a life well-lived—were gone. The physical loss was overwhelming, but it was the emotional toll that weighed heaviest. The life Luna had carefully built felt irreparably shattered.

For weeks, Luna struggled to make sense of what had happened. She moved into a temporary shelter, surrounded by others who had experienced the same tragedy. The initial days were filled with shock and despair, as she grappled with the question that haunted everyone around her: How do you rebuild when everything is gone? She felt paralyzed, unsure of where to begin.

But life often presents small openings even in the midst of devastation. One day, Luna noticed a sign at the shelter about a volunteer initiative to help rebuild the community. At first, the idea of helping others seemed impossible—she felt she had nothing left to give. Yet, something about the invitation stirred her. With tentative steps, she decided to attend the meeting.

The rebuilding initiative brought together neighbors, friends, and strangers, all united by a shared loss. Luna found herself surrounded by people who understood her pain in a way no one else could. Together, they rolled up their sleeves and began to clear debris, repair homes, and provide support for those most in need. The physical work was exhausting, but it gave Luna a sense of purpose she hadn't felt since the flood.

Through the initiative, Luna formed deep bonds with others who had also been displaced. They shared stories of loss, grief, and resilience, creating a network of mutual understanding and support. One elderly neighbor, Mr. Sharma, had lost not just his home but also his beloved garden, which he had tended for decades. Inspired by his heartbreak, Luna organized a small group to replant flowers and restore the garden. Watching Mr. Sharma smile as he held a blooming marigold in his hands was a moment of healing for them both.

As the weeks turned into months, Luna began to rebuild not just her home but also her sense of self. She discovered a hidden strength she hadn't known she possessed—a resilience that grew with each small victory. The act of giving back, of helping others find their footing, became a source of solace and empowerment. She started leading volunteer teams, inspiring others with her determination and optimism.

One day, Luna was invited to speak at a community gathering about her experience. Standing in front of her neighbors, she shared her journey from despair to hope, emphasizing the power of collective action and connection. Her words resonated deeply, reminding everyone that even in the face of unimaginable loss, rebuilding was possible—together.

Eventually, Luna's own home was restored, but the transformation she experienced went far beyond bricks and mortar. She became a pillar of her community, someone others turned to for guidance and encouragement. The disaster that had once left her broken became the foundation for a new chapter—one marked by purpose, connection, and an unwavering belief in the strength of the human spirit.

Takeaway:

Luna's story demonstrates that even in the wake of profound loss, rebuilding is possible through connection, purpose, and small, meaningful steps. By channeling her pain into action and supporting others, she not only restored her own life but also became a source of hope for her community. Her journey reminds us that the path to healing often begins with reaching out and taking the first step forward.

Practical Tip:

Identify one person or group you can reach out to today. Even small interactions, like joining a community event or online forum, can create a sense of belonging.

Principle 3: Small Steps Spark Change

Extreme challenges can feel paralyzing. But small, consistent actions—no matter how insignificant they may seem—create momentum.

Practical Tip:

Set micro-goals. For example:

Take a 10-minute walk to clear your mind.

Journal one positive moment from your day.

Research one new resource or opportunity that aligns with your needs.

Principle 4: Transform Pain into Purpose

Adversity can leave us questioning the meaning of our experiences. By finding ways to channel pain into purpose—advocacy, art, mentoring, or volunteering—we can create a new narrative for our lives.

Example: Malik's Advocacy Journey

Malik grew up in a neighborhood plagued by systemic inequality, where access to opportunities seemed like a distant dream. From a young age, he faced challenges that would test his resolve—underfunded schools, discriminatory practices, and limited resources. Despite his determination, the weight of these barriers often felt insurmountable. Then, an unjust incident changed everything.

Falsely accused of a minor crime, Malik spent months entangled in a legal battle that drained his family's finances and tested his spirit. The experience left him shaken, angry, and disillusioned. For a time, he withdrew from the world, feeling powerless against a system that seemed stacked against him. But as he processed his frustration, he realized he had a choice: he could either let the injustice define him or use it as a catalyst for change.

Taking that first step wasn't easy. Malik started small, attending community meetings and sharing his story with a local support group. His voice, raw with emotion, resonated with others who had faced similar struggles. Encouraged by their solidarity, Malik began volunteering with organizations advocating for criminal justice reform. He educated himself on policy, networked with activists, and even spoke at a town hall meeting—an act that once seemed impossible for someone as introverted as he had been.

As his confidence grew, so did his impact. Malik co-founded a grassroots initiative aimed at mentoring at-risk youth and advocating for systemic change. Through workshops and storytelling events, he empowered others to share their experiences and demand accountability. Every success—no matter how small—felt like a victory, not just for him but for his community.

Over time, Malik's journey transformed him. What began as a response to personal injustice became a mission to address broader societal inequities. His work gave him a renewed sense of agency, purpose, and hope. By channeling his pain into advocacy, Malik not only reclaimed his own balance but also became a beacon of change for others.

Takeaway:

Malik's journey illustrates the power of channeling personal adversity into collective action. By turning his pain into purpose, he not only found healing but also created ripples of hope and empowerment in his community. His story is a testament to the resilience of the human spirit and the transformative potential of advocacy in the face of systemic challenges.

Practical Strategies for Extreme Challenges

Create Anchors of Stability

Why It Matters: Stability provides the foundation for balance.

How to Start: List your most urgent needs and prioritize finding solutions, even temporary ones, for each.

Practice Grounding Techniques

Why It Matters: Traumatic experiences often make the present moment feel unbearable. Grounding techniques can help manage overwhelming emotions.

Exercise: Try the "5-4-3-2-1" technique: Identify 5 things you can see, 4 you can touch, 3 you can hear, 2 you can smell, and 1 you can taste.

Lean on Resilience Role Models

Why It Matters: Stories of others who've overcome adversity can inspire and guide you.

Example: Read memoirs, watch documentaries, or join support groups that share stories of resilience.

Focus on Meaningful Action

Why It Matters: Taking purposeful action, no matter how small, builds momentum and counters feelings of helplessness.

Example: Write down one thing you can do today to improve your situation or help someone else.

Seek Professional Support

Why It Matters: Therapists, counselors, or social workers can provide tools and guidance tailored to your challenges.

Example: David's Journey Through Homelessness

David's life once felt like a success story. A skilled chef, he had built a reputation for creating dishes that brought joy to countless diners. He loved his work, his small apartment, and the sense of stability he had carved out for himself. But life, unpredictable as it is, took an unexpected turn. A sudden illness led to mounting medical bills, forcing him to miss work and eventually lose his job. His savings vanished under the weight of these challenges, and before he knew it, David found himself on the streets with nothing but a worn backpack and a heart full of despair.

The first nights of homelessness were a blur of fear and shame. Sleeping on cold benches, scavenging for food, and trying to avoid the judgmental stares of strangers left David feeling invisible, like a shadow of the man he used to be. For weeks, he avoided shelters, too proud to accept help, and convinced that no one could understand the depths of his fall. Each day felt heavier than the last, and David began to lose hope that life could ever get better.

Everything changed when a kind stranger at a park handed him a flyer for a local nonprofit offering temporary housing. Reluctantly, and with nothing left to lose, David walked into their office. He expected pity but instead found compassion and understanding. For the first time in months, he felt seen. The organization provided him with a warm bed and meals, and in that moment, David realized he had been given something far more precious than shelter—he had been given a chance to rebuild.

David soon discovered the shelter had a kitchen where residents could volunteer. Nervous but eager to contribute, he offered to help. Stepping into the kitchen reignited something within him. Chopping vegetables, stirring pots, and plating food for others reminded him of his purpose—the ability to nourish and comfort through his craft. It wasn't just about the meals; it was about connection, sharing stories with others who were struggling, and finding a sense of belonging in the midst of adversity.

Months passed, and as David regained his footing, the nonprofit helped him secure an interview at a local diner. Armed with newfound confidence and a portfolio of volunteer work, David landed the job. It wasn't glamorous, but it was a step forward. Little by little, he saved enough to move into a modest apartment, marking the start of a new chapter. The same hands that had once prepared gourmet dishes were now crafting simple, hearty meals that brought smiles to customers' faces—and to his own.

But David's journey didn't stop there. Grateful for the second chance he'd been given, he began mentoring others at the shelter, sharing his story to inspire hope. He became a lifeline for those who felt the same despair he had once known, reminding them that setbacks, no matter how overwhelming, can be overcome with support, determination, and purpose.

Takeaway:

David's story is a powerful testament to the resilience of the human spirit. Through connection, compassion, and small steps forward, he found his way out of extreme adversity and rediscovered meaning in his life. His journey shows that even in the darkest moments, there is light to be found—and the possibility of building something beautiful from broken pieces.

When the Journey Feels Overwhelming

For those facing immense challenges, remember:

1. **You Are Not Alone:** Seek support from professionals, friends, or organizations.
2. **Focus on What You Can Control:** Even small actions can create ripples of change.
3. **Trust the Process:** Life's recalibration takes time, but growth is always possible.

Reflection Exercise: Finding Resilience

- Write about a moment when you faced adversity and overcame it.
- Reflect on what helped you through that time—your actions, support systems, or internal strengths.
- How can you apply those lessons to your current challenges?

Looking Ahead

In the next chapter, we'll explore how to proactively maintain balance even when life feels stable. You'll learn strategies for sustaining equilibrium, embracing growth, and finding contentment without waiting for life's next disruption.

Chapter 09

Proactively Building Balance

While setbacks and losses force us to recalibrate, waiting for life's disruptions to create balance isn't the only path forward. Instead, you can take a proactive approach to cultivating equilibrium in your daily life. By identifying what matters most, making thoughtful decisions, and nurturing your physical, emotional, and mental well-being, you can create a life that feels steady, meaningful, and resilient—even when challenges arise.

This chapter explores practical strategies for proactively building and maintaining balance, weaving in real-life examples and actionable exercises to guide you toward a more harmonious and fulfilling life.

The Power of Proactive Balance

Proactive balance is about creating stability before life demands it. Imagine a tightrope walker holding a balancing pole. Without the pole, the walker must constantly react to every wobble, risking a fall. With the pole, they can anticipate movements and maintain equilibrium with ease. Proactive balance is your balancing pole—it helps you navigate life's tightrope with confidence and poise.

Why Proactive Balance Matters

1. Prevents Extreme Imbalances

By addressing potential stressors early, you can avoid the extremes that lead to burnout, conflict, or stagnation.

2. Builds Resilience

Proactively cultivating balance strengthens your ability to handle setbacks when they arise.

3. Enhances Contentment

A balanced life allows you to savor the present moment while pursuing your goals with clarity and purpose.

Building Proactive Balance: Key Areas of Focus

1. Emotional Balance

Emotions are powerful but can throw you off course when unchecked. Proactively managing your emotional well-being helps you navigate challenges with clarity and composure.

Example: Fiona had always prided herself on being a hardworking professional and a devoted mother. But as the demands of her job intensified, she found herself carrying the stress of the office home. After long, grueling days, the smallest things—her children bickering over dinner or her husband's casual question about her day—would ignite her frustration. "Why can't they just understand I need some peace?" she thought, her voice sharp and her tone cold. Each outburst left her family walking on eggshells, and later, Fiona would sit alone in guilt, wondering why she couldn't control her emotions.

The tension in her home grew, the warmth replaced with an unspoken strain that broke her heart. One evening, after an argument over something trivial, Fiona saw her youngest daughter retreat quietly to her room with tears in her eyes. That moment hit Fiona hard. She realized her stress wasn't just affecting her—it was spilling over, hurting the people she loved the most.

Determined to change, Fiona began searching for ways to better understand and manage her emotions. She stumbled upon an article about mindfulness and decided to give it a try. At first, it felt strange to sit still, observing her thoughts without judgment. But over time, those 10 minutes each morning became her anchor—a sacred pause before the chaos of the day. She also started journaling at night, pouring her frustrations and fears onto paper, uncovering patterns in her emotional triggers she hadn't noticed before.

One day, after a particularly challenging meeting at work, Fiona came home exhausted. Her son spilled a glass of juice at dinner, and she felt the familiar wave of irritation rise. But this time, instead of snapping, she took a deep breath and walked to the sink, letting the moment pass. Later, as she helped him clean up, she noticed how grateful he looked, and it filled her with a quiet sense of pride. These small shifts became more frequent, and slowly, the atmosphere in her home began to change. The laughter returned, her children opened up to her again, and Fiona felt lighter—more in control of her emotions and more present with her family.

Strategies for Emotional Balance:

1. **Mindfulness Practices:** Dedicate 10 minutes daily to observing your thoughts and feelings without judgment. This practice helps create space between an emotional trigger and your reaction.
2. **Journaling:** Reflect on emotional patterns and triggers. Writing down your thoughts can provide clarity and insight into recurring stressors.
3. **Emotional Regulation Techniques:** Use deep breathing, visualization, or grounding exercises to calm your mind during challenging moments, allowing you to respond rather than react.

Takeaway: Fiona's journey shows that emotional balance doesn't mean eliminating stress—it's about managing it in a way that strengthens, rather than strains, your relationships. By prioritizing mindfulness and self-reflection, Fiona transformed her responses, bringing peace not only to herself but also to her family.

2. Physical Balance

Your body is the foundation of your life's balance. Neglecting physical well-being can disrupt every other area of your life, while nurturing it creates stability and vitality.

Example: Raj was the epitome of a driven entrepreneur. His startup had taken off, and with it came long hours, endless meetings, and the constant pressure to keep the momentum going. In his pursuit of success, Raj fell into a routine of skipping meals, grabbing fast food between calls, and sleeping only a few hours a night. Exercise became a distant memory. At first, he brushed off the signs—occasional headaches, fatigue, and irritability—but over time, his health began to take a serious toll. He found himself struggling to focus during meetings and snapping at his team over minor issues. The vibrant energy that once fueled his ambition seemed to have drained away.

The wake-up call came during a routine visit to his doctor, who warned him about his rising blood pressure and the potential long-term consequences of his lifestyle. "You're building your company, Raj, but at this rate, you're tearing yourself down," his doctor said. The words struck a chord. For the first time, Raj realized that his health wasn't just affecting him—it was jeopardizing his ability to lead, innovate, and even enjoy the success he had worked so hard for.

Determined to change, Raj began making small but meaningful adjustments. He started with a 20-minute walk each morning, a time he dedicated to clearing his mind and reconnecting with his surroundings.

At first, it felt like a chore, but soon it became his favorite part of the day. He replaced the coffee-fueled breakfasts with hearty, balanced meals, and his fast-food lunches with simple, nutritious options he prepared the night before. He also committed to going to bed by 10 p.m., ensuring he got at least seven hours of sleep.

The transformation was gradual but undeniable. Within weeks, Raj noticed he had more energy and sharper focus. He began to approach challenges with renewed clarity, making thoughtful decisions instead of reactive ones. His team noticed the change too—his calmer demeanor and increased patience lifted morale. Even his personal relationships benefited, as Raj had more energy to spend quality time with his family. For the first time in years, Raj felt not just successful but genuinely alive.

Strategies for Physical Balance:

1. **Prioritize Sleep:** Aim for 7–9 hours of restful sleep each night. A well-rested body and mind are crucial for energy, focus, and decision-making.
2. **Stay Active:** Incorporate daily movement, whether it's a brisk walk, yoga, or a favorite sport. Physical activity enhances both physical and mental well-being.
3. **Nourish Your Body:** Focus on whole, balanced meals to fuel your health. Plan ahead to avoid the pitfalls of convenience foods.

Takeaway: Raj's journey shows that physical balance isn't just about avoiding burnout—it's about creating a foundation of well-being that supports every other aspect of life. By prioritizing his health, Raj rediscovered the energy, focus, and joy that allowed him to thrive both personally and professionally.

3. Mental Balance

Mental clarity allows you to make thoughtful decisions and focus on what matters most. Proactively cultivating mental balance helps you manage stress, reduce overwhelm, and stay grounded.

Example: Evelyn had always considered herself a creative soul. Writing was her passion, and she cherished the quiet hours spent crafting vivid stories. But over time, her productivity waned. Each day, she'd sit down to write, only to be distracted by her phone—an endless stream of notifications, messages, and social media updates that pulled her away from her work. What should have been hours of creative flow turned into fragmented moments of frustration. Her unfinished drafts and mounting deadlines became a source of stress, and she began to doubt her ability to focus.

One evening, after another unproductive day, Evelyn reflected on how much time she had spent scrolling aimlessly. The realization was sobering. "If I can't even carve out an hour for myself," she thought, "how can I expect to bring my ideas to life?" Determined to reclaim her focus, Evelyn decided to make a change.

She started small, setting aside one hour each evening as a technology-free zone. She turned off notifications, placed her phone in another room, and created a dedicated writing space free from distractions. At first, the silence felt strange, even unsettling. She caught herself reaching for her phone out of habit, only to stop and remind herself why she had begun this journey. Gradually, the urge to check her phone faded, and in its place came a sense of clarity she hadn't felt in years.

As the weeks passed, Evelyn's writing began to flow effortlessly again. She finished drafts that had lingered untouched for months and even felt inspired to start new projects. The ideas that once seemed elusive now came freely, filling her with a renewed sense of purpose. Beyond her work, the mental clarity she gained spilled into other areas of her life. She felt more present in conversations, more mindful during daily routines, and more at peace with herself.

Strategies for Mental Balance:

1. **Digital Detox:** Set clear boundaries for technology use, such as screen-free evenings or dedicated times to check your devices.
2. **Declutter Your Mind:** Use tools like to-do lists or brain-dumps to organize your thoughts and reduce mental clutter.
3. **Lifelong Learning:** Engage in activities that challenge and stimulate your mind, such as reading, puzzles, or learning a new skill.

Takeaway: Evelyn's story shows the transformative power of mental balance. By stepping away from distractions and creating intentional space for her creativity, she not only rediscovered her passion but also enhanced her overall well-being. Her journey reminds us that focus is a skill worth cultivating, and sometimes, the simplest changes can lead to profound results.

4. Relational Balance

Your relationships play a crucial role in your life's harmony. Proactively investing in meaningful connections helps you create a supportive network that nurtures your well-being.

Example: Maeve had always valued her friendships, cherishing the shared laughter and support that defined her closest bonds. But as her career demands grew, her social life began to slip through the cracks. Meetings ran late, work trips consumed her weekends, and her phone was often filled with unanswered messages. Over time, she noticed an unsettling distance forming between her and her friends. Invitations to gatherings became less frequent, and when she did manage to meet someone, the connection felt strained.

One evening, as Maeve scrolled through photos of a recent get-together she had missed, a pang of regret washed over her. She realized how much she longed for those simple moments of camaraderie. Determined to rebuild her connections, Maeve decided to take action.

She started by reaching out individually to a few close friends, apologizing for her absence and expressing her desire to reconnect. Encouraged by their warm responses, she came up with an idea to bring everyone together regularly: monthly game nights. The first gathering was a modest affair, just a handful of friends laughing over board games and pizza. But the joy it brought was undeniable.

As the months passed, the game nights became a tradition, growing in size and significance. They weren't just evenings of fun—they were opportunities to share stories, celebrate milestones, and provide support during tough times. Maeve found herself looking forward to these moments, not as an obligation, but as a source of genuine happiness and renewal.

The effort to nurture her friendships had a profound impact. Maeve's sense of community deepened, and she noticed the positive ripple effects in her overall well-being. Her once-distant relationships became anchors of support, reminding her of the importance of prioritizing the people who matter most.

Strategies for Relational Balance:

1. **Nurture Key Relationships:** Schedule regular check-ins with loved ones, whether through calls, texts, or in-person meetups.
2. **Set Boundaries:** Protect your time and energy by saying no to relationships or commitments that drain you.
3. **Express Gratitude:** Show appreciation for the people who uplift and support you through thoughtful gestures or words.

Takeaway: Maeve's journey underscores the power of intentional connection. By prioritizing her friendships and creating space for shared experiences, she rediscovered the joy of community and strengthened the bonds that enriched her life. Her story reminds us that no matter how busy life gets, investing in relationships is always worth the effort.

5. Purposeful Balance

Living with purpose brings clarity and direction to your life. Aligning your actions with your values creates a sense of meaning that sustains you through challenges.

Example: Lena had spent years climbing the corporate ladder, pouring her energy into a high-pressure job that demanded long hours and constant output. Her achievements were impressive, but as the years passed, she began to feel an emptiness she couldn't ignore. The spark that had once driven her career had dimmed, leaving her questioning what all the hard work was truly for.

One day, after a particularly grueling week, Lena found herself at a park, watching children play and dogs chase frisbees. A simple interaction—a young girl laughing as her dog jumped joyfully—struck a chord in Lena. She realized how much she missed being part of something meaningful, something that connected her to others on a deeper level.

That weekend, she stumbled upon a flyer for a local animal shelter looking for volunteers. On a whim, she signed up, unsure of what to expect. Her first day was chaotic—walking excited, rambunctious dogs and cleaning cages—but it was also unexpectedly rewarding. By the end of her shift, Lena felt a sense of peace she hadn't experienced in years.

As weeks turned into months, her time at the shelter became a grounding force in her life. She discovered a passion for helping others, not just through her work with the animals but also in her interactions with fellow volunteers and the families adopting pets. The joy of giving back reminded her of values she had long sidelined: compassion, connection, and service.

Volunteering didn't just reignite Lena's sense of purpose—it created a ripple effect in other areas of her life. She approached her corporate job with renewed clarity, setting boundaries to ensure she had time for the things that truly mattered. Her relationships deepened, and her mental well-being improved. Lena's weekends at the shelter became more than a hobby; they became a cornerstone of a fulfilling, balanced life.

Strategies for Purposeful Balance:

1. **Clarify Your Values:** Reflect on what truly matters to you and let those values guide your decisions.
2. **Set Intentions:** Begin each day by identifying one action that aligns with your purpose, whether small or significant.
3. **Give Back:** Contribute to causes or communities that resonate with your values and bring meaning to your life.

Takeaway: Lena's journey highlights the transformative power of reconnecting with your purpose. By stepping outside her corporate bubble and engaging in meaningful work, she found fulfillment and balance that enriched every aspect of her life. Her story reminds us that even small steps toward purpose can create profound change.

Practical Exercises for Building Balance

Exercise 1: The Life Wheel

1. Draw a circle and divide it into segments representing different areas of your life (e.g., health, relationships, career, hobbies).
2. Rate your satisfaction in each area on a scale from 1 to 10.
3. Identify one action to improve balance in your lowest-rated area.

Exercise 2: Daily Balance Check-In

At the end of each day, ask yourself:

1. Did I take care of my emotional, physical, and mental well-being today?
2. Did I nurture my relationships?
3. Did I take one action aligned with my purpose?

Use this reflection to guide your actions for the following day.

Exercise 3: Gratitude Journal

1. Each day, write down three things you're grateful for and how they contribute to your balance.
2. Over time, this practice helps you appreciate the harmony in your life.

The Long-Term Benefits of Proactive Balance

1. **Reduces the Impact of Setbacks**A balanced life creates resilience, allowing you to navigate challenges with grace.
2. **Enhances Your Well-Being**Proactive habits nurture your physical, emotional, and mental health, creating a strong foundation for fulfillment.
3. **Fosters Deeper Connections**Relational and purposeful balance enriches your relationships and sense of belonging.
4. **Empowers Intentional Living**Aligning your actions with your values brings clarity, meaning, and contentment.

Looking Ahead

In the next chapter, we'll explore how to maintain balance during times of growth and success. You'll learn how to avoid the pitfalls of overexertion, stay grounded, and embrace sustainable progress.

Chapter 10

Maintaining Balance During Success

Success is often celebrated as the pinnacle of achievement, yet it brings its own set of challenges. While exhilarating, reaching new heights in your career, relationships, or personal goals often comes with increased demands, pressure to sustain momentum, and a risk of neglecting other aspects of life. Without careful attention, success can lead to burnout, inflated expectations, or unintentional imbalance.

This chapter explores how to maintain balance during times of growth and success. By grounding yourself in purpose, setting boundaries, and cultivating humility, you can fully enjoy your accomplishments while staying aligned with your values.

The Paradox of Success

Success, while rewarding, can disrupt balance in unexpected ways. It introduces:

1. **Increased Pressure**: The expectation to maintain or exceed your achievements.
2. **Neglected Areas**: Over-focusing on one aspect of life at the expense of others.
3. **Fear of Loss**: Anxiety about losing what you've worked so hard to gain.

Example:

For years, Rajiv had one goal: to climb the corporate ladder and achieve a long-coveted promotion. He poured himself into his work, often skipping family dinners and postponing vacations in the name of success. When the promotion finally came, it felt like a dream realized. The pride in his family's eyes and the congratulatory messages from colleagues made every sacrifice seem worth it.

But the honeymoon period was short-lived. The new role brought with it a mountain of responsibilities—endless meetings, tight deadlines, and the pressure to consistently outperform. Rajiv's workdays stretched into late nights, and weekends became an extension of his office hours. His once-vibrant family life began to fray. His partner grew distant, his children stopped sharing their little victories with him, and his health began to falter under the relentless stress.

What hurt the most was the realization that the very achievement he had worked so hard for was driving a wedge between him and the people he loved. The promotion, once a source of pride, became a source of regret. Rajiv felt trapped in a cycle where he was too busy to enjoy the fruits of his labor.

One evening, after missing his daughter's school play, Rajiv had a moment of clarity. Sitting alone in his office, he asked himself, *What's the point of success if it costs me everything I value?* That night, he resolved to make a change.

Rajiv began setting boundaries at work, delegating tasks, and prioritizing his family. He reclaimed his weekends for his loved ones and scheduled regular health check-ups. The shift wasn't easy—letting go of his workaholic habits felt unnatural at first—but over time, he found a rhythm that worked. His relationships began to heal, and he rediscovered the joy that had been missing in his life.

Takeaway: Rajiv's story illustrates the importance of balance during success. Without proactive measures, achievements can overshadow what truly matters. By recalibrating his priorities, Rajiv transformed his promotion from a source of stress into an accomplishment that enhanced, rather than detracted from, his life. His journey reminds us that success is most meaningful when it's in harmony with our values and well-being.

Strategies for Maintaining Balance During Success

1. Ground Yourself in Purpose

Success is most fulfilling when it aligns with your core values and long-term goals. By staying connected to your "why," you can navigate the pressures of success without losing sight of what matters most.

Example:

Lena had just achieved what many aspiring writers only dream of—her debut novel had become an instant bestseller. Invitations flooded in for her to speak at events, participate in book signings, and appear on panels. At first, Lena was exhilarated. The recognition and the chance to share her story with readers felt like a validation of her hard work and talent.

But as the weeks went by, the demands began to take a toll. Between planning her travel, preparing speeches, and managing media interviews, Lena found herself missing family dinners and quiet evenings at home. Her young daughter's bedtime stories were replaced by late-night flights, and her partner often ate dinner alone. Though the accolades were rewarding, Lena began to feel disconnected from the very people she held most dear.

One evening, after returning from yet another whirlwind trip, Lena sat on the edge of her daughter's bed, watching her sleep. It hit her:

the success she had worked so hard for was pulling her away from the life she wanted to live. She realized she needed to make a change.

Lena began setting clear boundaries around her commitments. Instead of saying yes to every opportunity, she became selective, choosing events that aligned with her goals and allowed her to stay present for her family. She prioritized virtual appearances over in-person travel whenever possible and blocked out time each week to focus solely on her loved ones. The result? Lena found a balance that allowed her to enjoy her newfound success without sacrificing her family life.

Practical Tip:

1. Regularly revisit your values. Ask yourself: *"Does this success align with the life I want to create?"*
2. When faced with opportunities, evaluate them not just for their professional benefits but also for their impact on your personal life.

2. Set Boundaries

Success often brings new demands on your time and energy. Setting clear boundaries protects your well-being and helps maintain balance.

Example:

Grace's business was booming, and she couldn't have been prouder. As a self-made entrepreneur, she had poured her heart and soul into her company, often working late into the night and sacrificing weekends to keep up with the growing demands. But as her business flourished, Grace began to feel the cracks in her personal life.

Her health started to decline—headaches from stress and sleepless nights became all too common. Family dinners turned into quick check-ins, and her friends started teasing her about being "impossible to reach." The realization hit her when her young son asked one evening, "Mom, are you ever going to play with me again?"

That moment stayed with Grace. She decided it was time to take back control of her schedule. She implemented a firm rule: no work after 6 PM. She communicated this boundary clearly to her team and even set an auto-reply for emails received after hours, letting clients know she would respond the next day.

At first, it was challenging. Grace felt a pang of guilt when she turned off her laptop and left tasks unfinished. But soon, she began to notice the benefits. Her evenings became a sacred space for family dinners, long walks, and reading before bed. Slowly, the tension she had carried for years began to melt away, replaced by a newfound sense of energy and clarity.

Her business didn't suffer—in fact, it thrived. Grace's decision to prioritize her well-being made her a better leader, allowing her to approach challenges with a calm and focused mind.

Practical Tip:

1. Create specific boundaries for work, relationships, and personal time.
2. Clearly communicate these boundaries to others and enforce them consistently.
3. Remember, boundaries are not limitations; they are the framework that sustains your success and well-being.

3. Celebrate Progress, Not Perfection

The pursuit of perfection can trap you in a cycle of stress and dissatisfaction. Shifting your focus to progress and growth ensures that you remain motivated without losing balance.

Example:

Gideon had always been an intensely driven athlete, with a trophy-lined shelf in his living room as evidence of his hard work. Yet, for every race he didn't win, the disappointment was unbearable. He would replay the events endlessly in his mind, scrutinizing every stride, wondering what he could have done differently. Over time, the joy he once felt when lacing up his running shoes turned into a knot of anxiety, and the sport he loved began to feel like a relentless test he was failing.

The turning point came after a particularly grueling half-marathon. Gideon didn't place, but for the first time, he didn't berate himself afterward. Instead, he noticed how much faster he had run compared to his last race. For the first time in years, he felt proud—not for beating others, but for beating his own limits.

Gideon began to shift his focus from the podium to the progress. He started tracking his personal bests, celebrating every incremental improvement. Whether it was shaving a few seconds off his time or conquering a tough training run, each milestone became a reason to feel proud.

This new mindset reignited Gideon's love for running. He realized it wasn't about standing on the podium—it was about standing taller in his own journey. With each step forward, the pressure faded, replaced by a deep sense of fulfillment and joy.

Practical Tip:

1. Keep a "progress journal" where you document milestones, lessons, and personal growth.
2. Reflect regularly on how far you've come, shifting your focus from external validation to personal satisfaction.
3. Remember, progress is the prize, and every step forward is worth celebrating.

4. Stay Humble

Success can inflate egos or create a sense of invincibility, disrupting balance. Cultivating humility keeps you grounded and fosters healthier relationships.

Example:

Zara had built her tech startup from the ground up, and it was growing rapidly. Investors were impressed, clients raved about the company's products, and accolades started pouring in. Zara was often in the spotlight, celebrated as the visionary behind the company's success. But Zara knew the truth—it wasn't just her leadership; it was the team she had carefully assembled.

Every product launch, every client deal, and every breakthrough was the result of late nights, collaborative brainstorming sessions, and the relentless efforts of her team. Zara made it a point to recognize this at every opportunity. Whether it was sending a heartfelt email after a successful project, publicly praising a team member during meetings, or taking everyone out to celebrate major milestones, she ensured that her gratitude was visible and genuine.

Her acknowledgment created an environment where people felt valued and motivated. Team members went above and beyond, not out of obligation but out of a shared sense of purpose and appreciation. Zara's humility and gratitude didn't just strengthen her team—it also anchored her in balance, reminding her that success wasn't a solo journey.

Practical Tip:

1. Regularly acknowledge the people and circumstances that contribute to your success.

2. Share credit generously—whether it's a simple thank-you note, a public acknowledgment, or a celebratory gesture.
3. Gratitude fosters connection, motivation, and a sense of shared accomplishment, creating a culture of balance and support.

5. Maintain Holistic Well-Being

Success in one area shouldn't come at the expense of others. By nurturing your physical, emotional, and relational health, you create a strong foundation to sustain growth.

Example:

Giselle's life felt like a whirlwind. As a new parent juggling a demanding job and a young baby, her days were packed with responsibilities. She often found herself drained by mid-morning, running on caffeine and sheer willpower. Despite her best efforts, she felt like she was falling short at both work and home.

One day, after an exhausting week, Giselle's mother gently suggested she take a few moments for herself. Hesitant at first, Giselle decided to try a simple morning walk before her baby woke up. The crisp air and quiet streets offered her a rare moment of peace, allowing her to clear her mind and recharge. She found herself returning home refreshed, ready to tackle the challenges of the day with renewed energy.

Over time, this small act of self-care became a cornerstone of Giselle's routine. It not only improved her physical health but also gave her the mental clarity to make better decisions and the emotional strength to be more present with her family. What started as a 10-minute stroll grew into a ritual that anchored her amidst the chaos, helping her achieve a healthier balance between work and home life.

Practical Tip:

1. Choose one self-care practice that resonates with you, such as exercise, meditation, or spending quality time with loved ones.
2. Start small and make it a consistent part of your daily routine—it's the small, sustainable habits that create lasting balance.

Examples of Sustained Success

1. The Balanced Artist

Anika had always poured her heart into her paintings, finding solace and joy in the process of creating. For years, she worked quietly, hoping her art would one day be recognized. That day came unexpectedly when one of her pieces went viral online. Overnight, she became a sensation, and commissions flooded in from around the world.

At first, Anika was elated. But as she began juggling numerous requests, she found her creative spark dimming. The joy she once felt while painting was replaced by the pressure to meet deadlines and satisfy clients' varying tastes. Her art felt more like a chore than an expression of her soul.

Realizing she was on the brink of burnout, Anika took a step back. She revisited her artistic vision and reminded herself why she had started painting in the first place. She made the bold decision to decline projects that didn't align with her style or values, focusing instead on pieces that resonated deeply with her. She also carved out time to experiment with new techniques and attend art workshops to nurture her growth.

This shift not only reignited her passion but also allowed her to maintain the quality and authenticity her audience admired. By prioritizing her long-term vision over short-term gains, Anika built a sustainable career that honored her love for art.

Lesson: Success is most meaningful when it supports your long-term vision rather than overwhelming you.

2. The Grounded CEO

Vikram had always been driven by ambition. As the CEO of a rapidly growing tech startup, his days were packed with back-to-back meetings, late-night brainstorming sessions, and constant decision-making. The company's success was soaring, but Vikram's personal life was crumbling under the weight of his demanding schedule. He missed important family milestones, and the little time he spent at home was overshadowed by exhaustion.

One evening, Vikram overheard his young daughter telling her mother, "Daddy's always too busy." The words stung deeply, forcing him to confront the cost of his relentless work ethic. He realized that while his efforts were building a thriving company, they were eroding the foundation of his personal life.

Determined to restore balance, Vikram made deliberate changes. He began scheduling weekly family dinners—no work calls, no interruptions—just quality time with his wife and children. He also implemented quarterly vacations, short getaways that allowed him to reconnect with his loved ones and recharge.

To his surprise, these small rituals didn't detract from his work; they enhanced it. Feeling more grounded and supported at home, Vikram brought renewed energy and clarity to his leadership. He became more attuned to his team's needs, fostering a workplace culture that valued well-being alongside productivity.

Lesson: Even in the most high-pressure roles, balance is crucial for sustainability. By prioritizing his personal life, Vikram discovered that success isn't just about professional achievements—it's about creating harmony across all areas of life.

Practical Exercises for Maintaining Balance

Exercise 1: The Success Map

Reflect on your recent successes. For each one, ask:

1. What values does this success align with?
2. What areas of my life might need more attention as a result?
3. What steps can I take to maintain balance moving forward?

Exercise 2: The Boundary Audit

- List the new demands on your time and energy arising from success.
- Identify which demands align with your priorities and which can be limited or delegated.
- Create a plan to enforce these boundaries.

Exercise 3: Gratitude in Success

1. Each week, write down three things you're grateful for in your journey. Reflect on how these contributions have shaped your success and sustained your balance.

The Ripple Effect of Balanced Success

Maintaining balance during success benefits not only you but also those around you. A balanced approach inspires others, strengthens relationships, and creates a legacy of sustainability and growth.

Looking Ahead

In the next chapter, we'll explore how to approach long-term growth without sacrificing balance. You'll learn how to embrace ambition while staying grounded, ensuring that your journey is as fulfilling as your destination.

Chapter 11

Embracing Sustainable Growth

Growth is an integral part of life, bringing purpose and fulfillment when pursued mindfully. Whether it's advancing your career, nurturing relationships, or honing personal skills, striving for improvement can enrich your journey. However, unchecked ambition can disrupt balance, leading to burnout, dissatisfaction, or a perpetual chase for more.

Sustainable growth offers a better way forward—a path that harmonizes ambition with well-being, ensuring that your aspirations align with your values and contribute to a meaningful, balanced life.

The Rhythm of Growth

Growth unfolds in cycles, much like the changing seasons. There are periods of:

- **Planting seeds**: Learning and preparation.
- **Nurturing growth**: Hard work and persistence.
- **Harvesting rewards**: Achievement and celebration.

Each phase is essential, and attempting to skip or rush any part of the cycle often leads to imbalance.

Example:

Aman was the embodiment of ambition. With a bold vision for his tech startup, he dove headfirst into the competitive market, determined to make his mark. Eager to expand quickly, he took on numerous projects, over hired staff, and pushed his team relentlessly, believing that speed was the key to staying ahead of the competition.

At first, the results were promising. Revenues surged, and the startup gained attention from investors. But beneath the surface, cracks were forming. Aman's team was overwhelmed, morale plummeted, and deadlines were increasingly missed. The rapid expansion strained the company's resources, leaving Aman juggling one crisis after another.

Two years in, the business faced a breaking point. Overworked and underprepared, the team couldn't sustain the relentless pace. Aman found himself staring at dwindling profits and an exhausted workforce. It was a harsh wake-up call.

Reflecting on the chaos, Aman recognized that his impatience had been his downfall. He began to recalibrate, focusing on sustainable growth instead of instant success. He streamlined projects, restructured his team, and prioritized their well-being with better workloads and regular check-ins. Slowly, the company stabilized, and Aman saw not just financial improvements but also a revitalized, committed team.

Takeaway: Growth isn't a race but a journey. Respecting the natural rhythm of growth creates a strong foundation for long-term success.

Principles of Sustainable Growth

1. Align Growth with Your Values

Growth is most fulfilling when it reflects your core values. Pursuing goals that contradict your values creates internal conflict and dissatisfaction.

Example:

Juniper had always been driven by ambition. As a corporate finance executive, she climbed the ladder swiftly, earning accolades, bonuses, and the admiration of her peers. On paper, her career was everything she had dreamed of. But deep down, Juniper felt an unshakable void.

Her days were consumed by spreadsheets, projections, and high-stakes meetings, yet she couldn't help but feel disconnected from the impact of her work. The thought gnawed at her: *Is this what I want my life to be about?*

One weekend, while volunteering at a local shelter, Juniper had a moment of clarity. Watching the direct impact her efforts had on people's lives brought a sense of fulfillment she hadn't experienced in years. It dawned on her that she was investing her energy in a career that didn't align with her deeper values.

After much soul-searching and planning, Juniper made a bold decision. She left her high-paying corporate job and joined a nonprofit organization focused on financial literacy for underserved communities. It was a challenging adjustment, but as she saw the tangible difference her work was making, Juniper felt a renewed sense of purpose. She wasn't just growing professionally—she was living a life that resonated with her core values.

Practical Tip:

Regularly revisit your goals and ask: "Does this align with the life I want to create?" Juniper's story reminds us that fulfillment comes not just from professional achievements but from aligning our actions with what truly matters to us.

2. Focus on Quality, Not Quantity

Chasing every opportunity can spread your energy thin. Prioritize depth and meaning over sheer breadth.

Example:

Lena had always been drawn to the vibrant world of art, fascinated by the endless possibilities it offered. When she decided to pursue a career as an artist, she dove headfirst into mastering every style she could—watercolor landscapes, hyper-realistic portraits, digital illustrations, and more. Her studio became a chaotic mix of unfinished projects, each screaming for her attention.

As the months passed, Lena found herself overwhelmed. The more she tried to excel in every style, the more her creative energy felt scattered and diluted. She started questioning her abilities and even doubted her passion for art.

One evening, while organizing her studio, Lena paused to admire an abstract painting she had created during a moment of spontaneous inspiration. Unlike her other works, it felt raw and deeply personal. Something about the interplay of colors and textures resonated with her.

That night, Lena decided to focus exclusively on abstract painting. By narrowing her scope, she discovered a sense of clarity and flow she hadn't felt in years. As she poured her heart into this singular style, her work began to attract attention. Galleries showcased her pieces, and collectors sought her out. More importantly, Lena felt deeply connected to her art—it was no longer about trying to prove herself but about expressing her unique perspective.

Practical Tip:

Identify the top three areas where you want to grow. Focus your time and energy on these priorities. Lena's journey shows that by embracing focus, you can channel your energy into what truly resonates, unlocking both satisfaction and success.

3. Celebrate Progress Along the Way

Appreciating the journey keeps you motivated and helps you savor the experience of growth.

Example:

Rahul had always dreamed of running a marathon, but the idea of completing 26.2 miles felt overwhelming. To build his confidence, he decided to break the journey into smaller, more manageable goals.

His first step was signing up for a local 5K race. Training for it was challenging, but the sense of accomplishment when he crossed the finish line was unmatched. Spurred by this success, he set his sights on a 10K race. Each week, as he added more distance to his runs, Rahul documented his progress in a journal. He noted not just the numbers—miles run, times recorded—but also the emotions he experienced: the thrill of a personal best, the pride of overcoming a tough training day, and even the occasional frustration.

When he finally completed his first marathon, it wasn't just about the race itself—it was about the journey that had led him there. Looking back through his progress journal, Rahul was reminded of how far he had come, both physically and mentally. Every milestone he had celebrated along the way made the marathon all the more meaningful.

Practical Tip:

Keep a "progress journal" to document achievements, lessons, and moments of joy. Celebrating milestones like Rahul did helps you stay motivated, appreciate your journey, and focus on the present.

4. Embrace Rest as a Growth Tool

Rest is not laziness—it's essential for sustainable growth. Like a field left fallow to restore its fertility, rest rejuvenates your capacity for effort.

Example:

Mira was a passionate teacher who had taken on the additional challenge of earning her master's degree. Determined to excel in both roles, she often stayed up late preparing lessons and studying. At first, she convinced herself that sacrificing sleep was a necessary trade-off for success.

But the effects soon caught up with her. Mira began feeling constantly exhausted, her focus wavered, and her performance at both work and school started to decline. She found herself snapping at her students over minor issues and struggling to retain information during her lectures. The harder she pushed herself, the more her productivity seemed to suffer.

One evening, after forgetting an important deadline, Mira realized she couldn't keep going this way. With support from a mentor, she restructured her schedule, prioritizing rest and setting boundaries for work and study time. She made it a rule to stop working by 9 PM, giving herself time to unwind and recharge. She also began incorporating short breaks throughout her day to reset her focus.

The change was almost immediate. With better rest, Mira found herself feeling sharper, more patient with her students, and better equipped to handle the demands of her coursework. Her grades improved, and her classroom became a space of renewed energy and enthusiasm.

Practical Tip:

Schedule regular rest periods and stick to them. Whether it's a fixed bedtime, a weekend break, or short daily pauses, treating rest as an integral part of your growth plan ensures sustained energy and focus.

5. Adapt to Change

Rigid plans can create frustration when faced with unexpected challenges. Flexibility allows growth to thrive in any circumstance.

Example:

Finn had ambitious plans to expand his family business, envisioning new stores across major cities. His vision was clear, and his team was ready to execute. But then the pandemic hit, forcing lockdowns and halting physical operations. Overnight, his meticulously crafted plans seemed impossible to achieve.

Initially, Finn felt overwhelmed and discouraged. The uncertainty of the situation and the financial strain on the business weighed heavily on him. Yet, he knew he couldn't afford to remain stagnant. Reflecting on the changing circumstances, Finn realized that the demand for online shopping was surging. Though it wasn't part of his original plan, he decided to pivot to digital marketing and build an online platform for the business.

The shift wasn't easy. Finn and his team worked tirelessly to create an e-commerce platform and develop a digital strategy to reach customers remotely. To his surprise, the move not only sustained the business but opened up a new customer base that extended far beyond his initial target markets. The digital platform became a core strength of the business, allowing it to thrive even after physical locations reopened.

Practical Tip:

When plans change, reframe challenges as opportunities. Ask yourself: *What possibilities does this situation reveal?* Adaptation often leads to unexpected growth and success.

Balancing Ambition and Contentment

Ambition drives you to grow, while contentment helps you savor where you are. Together, they create a powerful dynamic for sustainable growth.

The Ambition-Contentment Spectrum

Think of ambition and contentment as complementary forces. Striking a balance between them allows you to grow while appreciating your progress.

Example:

Meera, the CEO of a tech startup, was known for her visionary leadership and her ability to inspire her team. Under her guidance, the company achieved significant milestones, from launching groundbreaking products to securing substantial funding rounds. Yet, Meera was mindful of the pressures that came with relentless ambition. She had seen how unchecked growth could lead to burnout and dissatisfaction.

To foster a healthier work culture, Meera made it a point to celebrate every milestone, big or small. When her team launched a new product, she hosted a company-wide event to acknowledge their hard work and dedication. At the same time, she ensured that the company's goals remained realistic and achievable, setting an inspiring but manageable pace for growth.

Meera's balanced approach created a thriving workplace. Her team felt valued and motivated, knowing their achievements were recognized and their well-being prioritized. By aligning ambition with gratitude, Meera cultivated a culture of sustainable success.

Practical Tip:

Regularly reflect on both your achievements and your aspirations. Strive to ensure that ambition and gratitude coexist in harmony, fostering growth without sacrificing well-being.

Strategies for Sustainable Growth

1. Define Your Version of Success

Success means different things to different people. Clarify your personal definition to ensure your growth aligns with your unique vision.

Exercise:

Write down what success means to you in three areas: career, relationships, and personal growth. Reflect on whether your current goals align with this vision.

2. Prioritize Long-Term Goals

Short-term gains often come at the expense of sustainability. Focus on goals that build lasting fulfillment.

Exercise:

Create a vision board or list of long-term goals. Break them into smaller, actionable steps.

3. Practice Self-Compassion

Mistakes and setbacks are inevitable. Treat yourself with kindness to foster resilience and motivation.

Exercise:

Write a compassionate letter to yourself after a setback, acknowledging your efforts and encouraging perseverance.

4. Cultivate a Growth Mindset

View challenges as opportunities to learn. A growth mindset transforms obstacles into stepping stones.

Exercise:

Reflect on a recent challenge and ask: *"What did I learn from this experience?"*

5. Stay Connected to Your Community

Growth flourishes in a supportive environment. Engage with people who inspire and encourage your journey.

Exercise:

Join a group or network aligned with your goals, such as a professional association, hobby club, or mentorship program.

Examples of Sustainable Growth

1. The Patient Learner

Blake's dream was to become a renowned chef, but he knew that success in the culinary world wasn't built overnight. From his early days as a line cook in a bustling diner, Blake approached his craft with dedication and humility. He worked tirelessly to master the basics—perfecting the timing of a seared steak, understanding the delicate balance of flavors, and learning to manage the intense pace of a professional kitchen.

Over the years, Blake intentionally sought out opportunities to expand his skills. He worked in a variety of kitchens, each offering unique challenges and lessons. At a high-end French bistro, he learned the art of precision and plating, while a stint at a family-owned Italian restaurant taught him the value of simple, soulful cooking. Every experience deepened his understanding of the culinary arts and refined his vision for his own future restaurant.

But it wasn't just technical skills that Blake focused on. He paid close attention to the business side of the industry—how inventory was managed, how teams were motivated, and how a restaurant's atmosphere could make or break a dining experience. He kept a journal of ideas, inspirations, and lessons, knowing that each note would serve him when the time came to strike out on his own.

After nearly a decade of learning, saving, and planning, Blake finally felt ready to take the leap. With a clear vision and a well-thought-out business plan, he opened his first restaurant, a farm-to-table concept that combined the techniques he had honed with his passion for local, seasonal ingredients. The early days were challenging—long hours, unexpected setbacks, and the pressure of running a business—but Blake's patience and preparation paid off.

His restaurant quickly gained a loyal following, not because it was flashy or trendy, but because it offered consistently excellent food, a warm atmosphere, and a sense of authenticity. Blake's approach to growth remained steady and measured; instead of rushing to expand or chase fleeting trends, he focused on maintaining quality and building strong relationships with his customers and team.

Over time, Blake's reputation grew, and he earned accolades from food critics and industry peers. Yet, he never forgot the lessons of his journey: the importance of patience, preparation, and embracing growth at a sustainable pace. Blake's restaurant became not just a successful business, but a testament to the power of intentional, steady progress.

Lesson:

Blake's story illustrates that sustainable growth is built on a foundation of patience, preparation, and continuous learning. By taking the time to hone his craft, study his industry, and build a clear vision, Blake set himself up for long-term success. His journey reminds us that growth isn't about rushing to the finish line—it's about embracing the process, learning from every step, and laying a foundation that can withstand the test of time.

2. The Balanced Parent

Sonia had always been ambitious. As a marketing executive at a fast-growing company, she thrived on challenges and the sense of accomplishment her career brought. But Sonia was also a devoted mother to two young children, Maya and Arjun, who looked to her for guidance, love, and support. Balancing the demands of her career with the needs of her family often felt like walking a tightrope. At times, Sonia struggled with guilt—feeling like she wasn't giving enough to either her work or her children.

One evening, after missing her daughter's school play due to a last-minute work meeting, Sonia realized she needed to reassess her approach. The disappointment in Maya's eyes stayed with her, and Sonia vowed to find a better way to align her professional ambitions with her responsibilities as a parent.

Sonia began by setting clear boundaries at work. She committed to finishing tasks efficiently during office hours, delegating responsibilities where appropriate, and being transparent with her team about her family commitments. While it was difficult at first, she found that her colleagues respected her honesty and were willing to support her efforts to maintain balance.

At home, Sonia took a proactive approach to involve her children in her journey. Instead of shielding them from her work challenges, she began to share age-appropriate insights about her career. She explained the importance of teamwork, problem-solving, and perseverance, and even sought their advice on small matters, like picking designs for a campaign. Her children, curious and eager to help, felt a new sense of connection to her professional world.

To further strengthen their bond, Sonia created dedicated family time. Friday evenings became "family fun nights," where the focus was on games, storytelling, or cooking together—no interruptions allowed. These moments became cherished rituals that grounded her, even during hectic work weeks.

Sonia's approach began to pay off. At work, her clear boundaries and efficient communication earned her respect and admiration, leading to a well-deserved promotion. At home, her children thrived under her attention and involvement. Maya started sharing her own aspirations with Sonia, inspired by her mother's example, and Arjun proudly told his classmates about the "cool projects" his mom worked on.

While the journey wasn't without its challenges—occasional late nights or missed events—Sonia discovered a rhythm that allowed her to advance in her career while nurturing her family. Most importantly, she realized that balance didn't mean doing everything perfectly; it meant being present and intentional in every role she played.

Lesson:

Sonia's story demonstrates that balance is achievable, even in the face of competing demands, through clear boundaries, intentional time management, and genuine connection. By involving her children in her journey and prioritizing quality moments with them, she fostered mutual respect and understanding. Sonia's experience reminds us that balance is not about having it all—it's about creating harmony between your commitments and your values, one intentional step at a time.

Sustainable Growth and the Framework

The dynamic balance framework supports sustainable growth by emphasizing:

1. **Purpose**: Aligning growth with your values ensures fulfillment.

2. **Equilibrium**: Balancing ambition with rest prevents burnout.
3. **Resilience**: Adapting to setbacks fosters long-term progress.

Looking Ahead

In the final chapter, we'll explore how to integrate the framework into your daily life. You'll learn how to make balance a guiding principle, creating a life of resilience, fulfillment, and harmony.

Chapter 12

Living a Balanced Life

As we conclude this journey, the question remains: How do you integrate the principles of balance into your daily life? The ideas we've explored—embracing setbacks as recalibrations, letting go of comparison, sustaining balance during success, and pursuing sustainable growth—are not abstract concepts. They are practical, actionable tools designed to create a life of harmony, resilience, and fulfillment.

This final chapter ties everything together, showing you how to make balance not just an occasional goal but a guiding principle in your everyday existence.

The Essence of a Balanced Life

Living a balanced life doesn't mean avoiding challenges or suppressing ambition. It means engaging fully with life's highs and lows while fostering stability, alignment, and meaning. Balance is not a fixed state or a final destination—it's a dynamic process of continuous recalibration, reflecting your evolving goals, values, and circumstances.

Guiding Principles for a Balanced Life

1. Balance is Dynamic, Not Static

Life is ever-changing, and balance requires adaptability. Like a tightrope walker who constantly adjusts to stay steady, you must remain flexible in response to shifting circumstances.

Example:

When Ivy became a first-time parent, she was determined not to let motherhood disrupt her career. She tried to maintain the same demanding work routine she had before her baby arrived—late nights, packed schedules, and endless to-do lists. But the balancing act quickly became unsustainable. Ivy felt torn between her work responsibilities and the needs of her newborn, leaving her overwhelmed and emotionally drained.

One evening, after missing yet another bedtime story with her baby, Ivy broke down and realized something had to change. She took a step back and reassessed her priorities. Instead of fighting to maintain her old routine, she decided to design a new one that reflected her evolving life. She adjusted her work hours, delegated tasks, and carved out dedicated family time.

The changes weren't easy, but over time, Ivy found a rhythm that worked. She began to feel more present in both her personal and professional life. Her career continued to thrive—not in spite of the changes, but because of the renewed clarity and focus they brought her.

Takeaway:

Embrace life's transitions as opportunities to recalibrate. Balance isn't about rigidly clinging to old routines—it's about adapting to what truly works in the present, honoring both your needs and your priorities.

2. Balance is Personal

Your version of balance is as unique as your fingerprint. What works for others may not work for you, and that's okay.

Example:

Ronan was in his element in a fast-paced corporate environment. He thrived on tight deadlines, quick decisions, and the adrenaline of a high-stakes career. His energy was contagious, and he drew inspiration from the dynamic nature of his work. Meanwhile, Lena, his friend from college, took a completely different approach. She preferred a slower, more reflective path, building her career in academia where she could deeply immerse herself in research and teaching.

At one point, both found themselves questioning their choices. Ronan wondered if he was missing out on deeper, more contemplative work, while Lena sometimes felt pressured to pursue more visible and rapid achievements like her peers. A candid conversation between the two revealed their shared struggles, but it also reminded them of the importance of honoring their unique preferences.

Instead of comparing themselves to others—or to each other—they leaned into their strengths. Ronan embraced his love for the fast-paced world of corporate strategy, while Lena found fulfillment in the quiet impact of her academic contributions. Both realized that their paths, while vastly different, were equally valid and fulfilling.

Takeaway:

Define what balance means for you. Trust your individual preferences and priorities, even if they diverge from societal norms or the paths of others. Balance is deeply personal, and your unique approach is what makes your journey meaningful.

3. Balance Requires Intentionality

A balanced life doesn't happen by chance. It requires conscious effort, reflection, and a willingness to prioritize what matters most.

Example:

Aria had always been a go-getter, juggling a demanding job, personal commitments, and her passion for painting. But over time, the constant hustle began to take its toll. She often felt frazzled, unsure if her energy was being spent on things that truly mattered. One evening, after a particularly exhausting week, Aria decided she needed a change.

She started a simple ritual: every Sunday evening, she set aside 30 minutes for a personal check-in. With a cup of tea and her journal, she asked herself three questions:

1. What went well this week?
2. What felt off-balance?
3. What adjustments can I make next week?

At first, the process felt unfamiliar, but it quickly became her favorite part of the week. She began noticing patterns—like how overloading her weekdays left her feeling drained by Friday. With this awareness, she started blocking out time for rest and prioritizing tasks that aligned with her long-term goals.

Over time, Aria's self-check-ins transformed her approach to life. They didn't just keep her balanced—they gave her clarity, helping her live more intentionally and authentically.

Takeaway:

Build intentional habits that support balance, such as regular self-reflection or mindful goal-setting. Simple practices like Aria's weekly check-in can help you stay aligned with your values and make informed adjustments. Balance thrives on awareness and intentionality.

Practical Practices for Living a Balanced Life

1. Start Each Day with Intention

Setting a daily intention creates focus and clarity, helping you align your actions with your values.

Exercise:

Each morning, write down one intention for the day, such as:

1. "Today, I will prioritize meaningful connections."
2. "Today, I will approach challenges with curiosity."

2. Make Micro-Adjustments

Big changes can feel daunting, but small, consistent actions create lasting transformation.

Exercise:

Identify one small adjustment you can make each day to enhance balance. For example:

1. Take a 10-minute walk to clear your mind.
2. Spend 5 minutes expressing gratitude.
3. Dedicate 15 minutes to a hobby or passion.

3. Reflect and Recalibrate Regularly

Periodic reflection keeps you attuned to your needs and helps you make informed adjustments.

Exercise:

At the end of each week, ask yourself:

1. What went well this week?
2. What felt unbalanced?

3. What adjustments can I make for next week?

4. Cultivate Resilience

Resilience—the ability to bounce back from setbacks—is the foundation of a balanced life.

Exercise:

Reframe challenges as opportunities. For example, instead of viewing a missed deadline as a failure, consider what it taught you about time management or prioritization.

5. Celebrate Progress, Not Perfection

Acknowledge your growth, no matter how small. Celebrating progress reinforces a positive mindset and builds motivation.

Exercise:

Create a "celebration jar." Each time you achieve a goal or overcome a challenge, write it down and place it in the jar. Periodically review these notes to appreciate your journey.

Gratitude: The Anchor of Balance

Gratitude shifts your perspective from what's lacking to what's abundant. It's a grounding force that enhances your ability to maintain balance.

Example:

Hugo's days were often a blur of meetings, deadlines, and endless to-do lists. He frequently ended the day feeling drained, his mind fixated on what hadn't gone right—a missed opportunity, an unresolved problem, or a task left undone. The constant focus on what was lacking left him restless and dissatisfied.

One evening, during a conversation with a friend, Hugo learned about the power of gratitude. Intrigued but skeptical, he decided to give it a try. He started small: each night, before going to bed, he wrote down three things he was grateful for in a small notebook by his bedside.

At first, it felt forced. Some days, all he could muster was gratitude for his morning coffee or the fact that it didn't rain. But as the days turned into weeks, something shifted. Hugo began noticing the small, beautiful moments he had overlooked—a meaningful conversation with a colleague, a smile from a stranger, or the way the evening sun bathed his living room in golden light.

His gratitude practice became a nightly ritual. Over time, Hugo noticed a profound change in his perspective. Instead of focusing on what went wrong, he began to see the abundance of good in his life. The practice didn't eliminate his challenges, but it gave him the resilience and optimism to face them with a lighter heart.

Practical Tip:

Start a gratitude journal or set aside time daily to reflect on what you appreciate. Whether it's a meaningful conversation, a moment of laughter, or a beautiful sunset, focusing on the positives can reinforce your sense of balance and well-being.

The Ripple Effect of Living a Balanced Life

When you commit to balance, the impact extends beyond yourself. Your well-being influences your relationships, work environment, and community, creating a ripple effect of positivity and harmony.

Example:

Lena, a manager at a growing firm, was no stranger to the demands of her role. In her earlier years, she often sacrificed sleep and personal time to meet tight deadlines, believing that relentless effort was the key to success. But as her team grew, Lena noticed the toll her habits took—not just on her but on her colleagues, who mirrored her behavior. Burnout became a recurring issue, morale plummeted, and productivity suffered.

Determined to make a change, Lena began modeling a more balanced approach. She set clear boundaries, refusing to send emails after hours and taking time to recharge. She encouraged her team to prioritize self-care, even instituting wellness initiatives like regular check-ins and flexible schedules.

The shift was palpable. Inspired by Lena's example, her team adopted healthier work habits, leading to a noticeable improvement in morale and collaboration. Productivity soared, but more importantly, the workplace became a supportive environment where people felt valued and energized.

Takeaway:

Your dedication to balance can inspire and uplift others, fostering a culture of well-being in your community. When you prioritize harmony in your life, you lead by example, creating a ripple effect of positivity that extends far beyond your immediate circle.

Integrating Balance into Everyday Life

To live a balanced life:

1. **Reframe Challenges**: View obstacles as recalibrations, not failures.
2. **Focus on Your Path**: Let go of comparisons and trust your unique journey.
3. **Embrace Dynamic Growth**: Pursue meaningful goals while maintaining equilibrium.

4. **Celebrate the Present**: Recognize and honor the harmony you've cultivated.

Closing Exercise: The Balance Manifesto

Craft a personal manifesto to solidify your commitment to balance. Include:

1. Your core values.
2. Your vision for a balanced life.
3. The practices you'll embrace to sustain harmony.

Revisit this manifesto regularly as a reminder of your intentions and progress.

A Final Thought

Life is a dynamic and ever-evolving journey. By embracing the framework of balance, you can navigate its twists and turns with clarity, resilience, and purpose. While the path may not always be easy, it will always be meaningful—because it is uniquely yours.

Live your life as a dance between ambition and contentment, growth and rest, and action and reflection. Balance isn't just a goal; it's a way of being, a lens through which you experience the fullness of life.

Conclusion: Balance is All You Need

As you close this book, take a moment to reflect on the journey we've shared. Together, we've explored the dynamic interplay of free will and fate, the recalibration of setbacks, the dangers of comparison, and the joys of sustainable growth. Each chapter has offered tools and insights to help you embrace balance as a guiding principle in your life.

Balance is not a rigid formula—it's a living, breathing process. Imagine your life as a symphony, where every experience, whether triumphant or painful, contributes to its melody. Balance is the unseen conductor, guiding each note into harmony. It's about listening to your inner compass, staying aligned with your values, and adjusting gracefully to life's ever-changing rhythms. Whether you're navigating moments of challenge, celebrating success, or pursuing growth, balance is your foundation—a source of strength, clarity, and fulfillment.

The Gift of Balance

Living a balanced life isn't about achieving perfection. It's about creating harmony between the opposing forces that shape your journey. It's about finding meaning in every experience—joyful or painful—and trusting that life's recalibrations are always working for your highest good.

Balance allows you to:

- Face setbacks with resilience and grace.
- Celebrate your unique path, free from the weight of comparison.

- Pursue growth with purpose and sustainability.
- Cultivate gratitude for the present while building a brighter future.

Like the symphony of your life, balance transforms challenges into stepping stones and achievements into moments of shared joy. When you choose balance, you're not just creating a better life for yourself—you're inspiring those around you to do the same. Your ripple effect has the power to transform relationships, communities, and beyond.

Your Balanced Life Awaits

The real work begins now. Take what resonates from this book and start small. Choose one practice, one mindset shift, or one intentional action to integrate into your daily life. Trust the process, and give yourself permission to grow at your own pace. Balance is not something you find—it's something you cultivate, step by step, choice by choice.

This book isn't just a guide—it's a companion for your path. Revisit its lessons as often as needed, and trust that balance is not a destination but a journey—a dance with life's unpredictability that creates meaning and harmony along the way.

A Closing Thought

Life's journey is unique for each of us, shaped by individual struggles and triumphs. Whether you're managing a low-paid job, dealing with unemployment, grieving a profound loss, navigating the uncertainties of a single-income household, or simply feeling adrift in a life that lacks meaning, know this: your challenges, while uniquely yours, are not insurmountable.

This book's framework of dynamic calibration is not a quick fix, but a guide—a way to see beyond the present struggle, to understand that life is always working quietly in the background to restore balance and lead you toward growth and fulfillment. Your journey might not look like anyone else's, but it is no less meaningful, and its recalibration is always at work.

Here's the truth: Life is not a single story; it is a series of chapters. Some are filled with joy and accomplishment, while others are shadowed by grief and uncertainty. But every chapter is necessary to the larger story of who you are becoming. Your current challenges are not the end of your story—they are the tension points that make the resolution even more powerful.

Even in your darkest moments, when hope seems distant, small acts—showing up, reaching out, making one small decision to keep moving—can begin to tip the scales. You may not see the immediate effects, but each step contributes to a greater recalibration. Every choice to persevere is a vote of confidence in the process of life.

Remember, life's balance is not about achieving perfection or avoiding struggles altogether. It's about trusting that, no matter how off-kilter things may feel right now, there is always a pathway toward balance and purpose. The seeds of growth are often planted in the soil of adversity, and it is through time, patience, and trust in life's calibration process that those seeds bloom into something beautiful and enduring.

As you close this book, take this thought with you: The dynamic calibration process is always active, always working to guide you back to equilibrium—even if you can't see it yet. By embracing small steps, staying engaged, and trusting the process, you're paving the way toward a brighter chapter filled with renewed purpose and balance.

You are resilient, your journey is meaningful, and your future is a canvas waiting for your brushstrokes. Trust in life's recalibration, and allow yourself to grow into the masterpiece that only you can create.